DEAR ACCOUNTANT

Dear Accountant

Stories, Advice, and Explorations

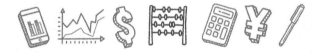

Cecilia Leung, CPA

LIONCREST
PUBLISHING

DEAR ACCOUNTANT
Stories, Advice, and Explorations

ISBN   978-1-5445-2114-5   *Hardcover*
       978-1-5445-2113-8   *Paperback*
       978-1-5445-2112-1   *Ebook*

Dedicated to all the accountants in the world.
The world is so big and full of infinite possibilities.
Explore it and have fun!

Remember: the work that we do matters. You matter!

Dear Tina,
   I'm so excited to get to know you.
You are kind and intelligent, and I wish
you all the best, in your amazing and
incredible journey ahead!

                              Cece
                              July 2022

Contents

Foreword

In my own career—whether as a CEO, as a board member of a public, private, or nonprofit organization, or when advising C-suite executives—I am keenly aware of the necessity of understanding "the numbers," insights that ultimately derive from the work of accountants. Whether it is from the CFO, the controller, the staff accountants, or external accounting consultants, the fuel that drives the decision-making comes from understanding how the businesses or organizations are doing, and that begins with understanding the financial statements. The field of accounting is to business what medicine is to the healthy survival of people; it is the way to diagnose and then set a course toward thriving. The appreciation that I have for the work of the accounting profession is something that has developed over the course of many decades, and getting to know Cecilia has been a catalyst in that journey.

I had the pleasure of getting to know Cecilia many years ago when we were both working at JP Morgan. I was the chief marketing officer at the time, and Cecilia was a controller in the Private Bank. We immediately connected, and her curiosity, desire to grow personally and professionally, and passion for her work was clear, and something I continue to admire about her today.

I am not sure I know anyone who sets a goal and goes after it in a more focused and dedicated way than Cecilia, which is why, in addition to her tremendous career success, she is also an accomplished pianist, author, business owner, and even an athlete. She is one of the most interesting people I know. I recall a number of years ago receiving a message from Cecilia when she had exhaustedly and victoriously reported her achievement of "Everesting," a multi-day hike up and down a mountain in Vermont where the sum of the amount hiked equals scaling Everest. She had decided to do this, and for her, that means it was as good as done. That same discipline came to bear when she decided it was important to provide a different kind of lens into the multidimensional and deeply interesting work that she, and others, have done in the world of accounting. Interesting accounting work may seem like an oxymoron, but it won't once you have finished reading the stories contained in this completely new look at a very old profession.

I am excited that her passion for the field of accounting has brought her to bring this book to fruition. I have seen it as an act of love—love for putting the pieces together and painting a picture of deep insights to make businesses run better, but more importantly, love for the people who do this work. Her desire to share, and to help people avoid pitfalls and make more informed decisions, yielded this wonderful book you are now holding. Whether you are trying to decide if accounting is for you, or you are already in the field and wondering where it can take you, I am confident that you will find the answers you are looking for, and much more, in this volume. I am honored to be a part of it, and to know the incredible woman who made it happen!

There are times in our lives when we all need a Sherpa. Someone to guide us through the trials and travails of life—or help us reach new heights. I love this book because Cecilia has created a carefully crafted beacon for accountants at all stages of their careers to gain wisdom and insights that will facilitate that growth. I can't think of anyone better suited to bring this all together than Cecilia.

—Catherine Flax

MANAGING DIRECTOR AT CRA, INC.,

FORMER SENIOR EXECUTIVE AT JP MORGAN

NEW YORK CITY, NEW YORK

Preface

Over the years, I have had the privilege of mentoring many young, bright, ambitious professionals like you. I am often reminded of my younger self—feeling overwhelmed, insecure, and confused about the future.

In the course of my work, I also speak with many successful and established professionals, like some in this book, who unfortunately did not experience the advantages of mentorship. Instead, they felt the frustration of having to figure things out on their own, often wondering how much easier it might have been to navigate their career path had they received the proper guidance and encouragement.

We all wish we knew then what we know now.

This is why I have made it my vocation to help young, aspiring accounting professionals like you build confidence and competence, and be more strategic, intentional, and prepared in advancing your career in order to live more fulfilling and meaningful lives.

As the inspiring African proverb advises, "If you want to go fast, go alone. If you want to go far, go together." My intention is to build an ever-growing community of young, determined accounting professionals, all embarking on their journey *together*, encouraging each other to go far in their careers.

My sincerest wish is that this book becomes the first step in your journey. Together, we can, and will, have a positive impact in our profession and in the world, while creating a vibrant community in which generations of future accounting professionals may thrive.

I would like to invite you to stay connected with me, and other fellow and aspiring accounting and finance professionals in the *Dear Accountant* community, at *www.dearaccountantbook.com*.

Introduction

I am proud of my profession. A CPA career isn't easy. Whether you're just learning about it in school or you've started your career, you know how much work goes into succeeding. Despite the vast number of amazing, unique, and inspiring individuals who make careers as CPAs, we can never seem to outshine the stereotypes. Why can't we get positive representation in movies or TV shows about accountants? Doctors, lawyers, and tech giants always find themselves in the spotlight, showing their range of talents, passions, and brilliant thoughts. For accountants, the most attention we get from the general public is once a year when people file their taxes or do bookkeeping. As an industry, we have evolved graciously beyond that!

If you really pause and think for a moment—accountants are everywhere. Accounting touches many aspects of our life. There are educators, tax strategists, forensic accountants, finance executives, entrepreneurs, and so many more. Smart, innovative professionals are teaching and training the next generations of accountants, protecting public interests, helping individuals and businesses save money and build wealth, investigating and catching bad guys who commit fraud, and playing a critical role in closing mergers and acquisitions (M&A), initial public offering (IPO) deals, and beyond.

Beyond the Numbers and Stereotypes

Accounting is more than just numbers. It's also the understanding of the function of money and how money works. The foundations of financial literacy allow us to see a big picture of how money flows in and out, and how to budget, save, and invest. Great accountants are able to connect the concepts and fundamentals of finance, business, and economics together to reach a better understanding of numbers and what to do with them.

Accounting is often called the language of business. It acts as the lifeblood of a business, flowing through different departments, ultimately leading to the head of the business. Accountants help interpret and present numbers to clients to provide insights about the past, present, and future health of an organization or company and connect all sides of the business.

The traditional accountant stereotype is of an analytical, organized, detailed-oriented, and nerdy bean counter who only talks in math equations and crunches numbers all day. I think those are cool personality traits. In fact, I want to be that person's best friend!

Navigating Your Career Journey

No Roadmap or Playbook for a Perfect Career

No roadmap or playbook exists for a perfect career, and no perfect career (whatever that may look like to you) promises a perfect life. Your life is made up of all the incredibly complex scenarios that you have to solve. Luckily for you, accountants are great at complex problem-solving.

Although work ethic and strong skills are important (and no one can ever take that away from you), there are many other aspects that impact your career, such as the general economy and current events, which are entirely out of our control. When something does or does not happen, we often ask why. Did we not try hard enough? What went wrong? Next time you find yourself asking why, reflect on the idea that perhaps the answers are not easily found. In fact, you will never know where any seemingly "bad" experience is going to take you. Many times, it is just a blessing in disguise! Many external factors—such as your encounters, people, timing, environment, and opportunities—may determine the outcome of an event. Whether or not you get a job offer or promotion can be dependent on many external and subjective factors. How far you can reach, and rise, is often due to reasons that are beyond your work performance or your credentials. All the right factors have to be aligned at the same time for things to pan out. While you should actively take advantage of all that is under your control, remember not to worry about what you cannot control.

Enjoy the Journey and Discover Yourself

When chasing career aspirations, it's easy to forget that life is made up of so much more than your job description. Your career, while important, is really only a small part of your life; other aspects of your life—well-being, relationships, art, or however you choose to fill your time—will create your unique journey. Academic or professional success and failure will exist alongside love and heartbreak, and will together produce your life experiences. Your experiences become your stories, and each uniquely contributes to the creation of your journey.

As unique individuals, we each experience exclusively personal versions of life. We make our own choices based on what we know best at the time. Accounting is a skill, and becoming an accountant is just the beginning. There are so many options within accounting—so much so that how you use the accounting skill to make a positive impact will be entirely up to you. An accountant's career can be an incredibly fulfilling and meaningful journey. We keep on learning and growing while forming our values and beliefs. Our characters are continuously being tested through challenges and adversities within the field, especially in our field, since the public relies heavily on our ethics to do the right thing and protect them.

Ultimately, an accountant's journey is never simply about making money, getting by in life, or moving up the corporate ladder. It is about who we become in the process as an individual and as a professional, working toward our fullest and greatest potential, continuing to help others, and making this world a better place.

Who Am I and Why Did I Write This Book?

The Power of Mentoring and Coaching

The purpose of this book is to provide young people with guidance through the world of accounting they might not have access to through school or work colleagues. I started mentoring others when I volunteered in a community center in my first year of college. Being able to share my own journey with young people, and demonstrating that not every life path is perfect, gave me so much joy and fulfillment. I truly believe that you can succeed despite deep struggles or uncertainty.

Over the past 2 decades, I have been fortunate to mentor many young, bright, and ambitious individuals from different backgrounds, personalities, aspirations, hopes, and dreams. Their journeys always remind me of my own. Mentors should always be finding ways to help individuals who generally don't get a lot of guidance—underprivileged kids coming from low-income families, some without parents, immigrants who navigate a world they can't always understand, and individuals with different abilities, struggling to find their place. I have learned so much from my mentees and am humbled to have seen so many people from all walks of life grow and evolve over the years.

Our legacy is what we do every day, every life we have touched, and every person whose life was helped and changed. I am so grateful to see my mentees exploring accounting, honing their practical skills, and growing their confidence as they figure out their role as contributors to society and the world. That's the very reason why I am motivated to continue to do this work in mentoring, and another reason I am excited about publishing this book.

I am forever grateful for the people who have helped me along the way to get to where I am today. I believe that we all have tremendous power and potential; perhaps we just need an extra push and vote of confidence every so often to know that someone believes in us. I seek new mentors with every transition I make in my professional career: moving to a new country, school, industry, or job becomes a lot more manageable when a caring soul is cheering you on from the sidelines.

This book is one of my many ways to pay it forward for our future accounting leaders. My first piece of advice is to encourage you to do the same; continue to pay it forward and help others as you might have been helped along the journey. The world is big, with limitless opportunities waiting for you to discover! It's easy to make assumptions about successful and accomplished people, but through their journeys you'll learn that nothing is easy, and everyone has their share of struggles and obstacles to overcome. I hope you'll find confidence and optimism in your career path knowing that we have all gone through what's ahead of you. *Know* that we are just like you—if we can do it, you can too!

My Career Journey

1

Beyond the Numbers

Defy the Stereotypes and Create My Own Myth

Cecilia Leung

**FOUNDER OF THE ENTREPRENEUR CFO,
AUTHOR, AND PODCAST HOST**

When I was a kid, I thought my life was destined to look exactly like the lives of those around me. I never imagined I could create my own future. I certainly had no idea I could live a life as fulfilling as the one I have now. Without a sense of direction or desire to emulate the lives I was most familiar with, I would often escape to books and movies. They allowed me to expand my imagination, and in some way, escape the realities I was struggling with. I wasn't lacking in basic needs, but I was struggling to find my place.

I was born and raised in the '80s in the vibrant city of Hong Kong. For over 100 years before Hong Kong was handed back to China in 1997, it was a thriving colony under British governance. Life was good; the economy, businesses, and middle class were all thriving. It created the perfect backdrop for a happy childhood. I had the best memories from my kindergarten days; I remember wanting to grow up to be a kindergarten teacher so I could stay in that happy place forever.

And then suddenly, although I wasn't sure why, that happiness started to fade as I entered into first grade. I had friends, but I remember feeling out of place and alone—in reality, and in my thoughts. I am Chinese, but I barely looked like the typical Chinese girl—I was a bit chubby with tanned skin, big thick hair, and a big nose. Kids made fun of me because I looked different than them. I tried very hard to be like everyone else, despite knowing it was impossible for me. I often wondered why it was so wrong to be different. Why did I have to be the same to be liked or accepted? I laugh about it now, but it was hurtful to my younger self. I just wanted to fit in.

The Asian Girl Who Failed Math

Growing up in an Asian family, our expectations were clear and straightforward: Respect and obey our parents and elders. Do well in school and extracurricular activities. And, of course, make our family proud. I managed to meet the standards required of me by doing well in both academics and extracurricular activities until the fifth grade. After that, the school environment was extremely stressful. I got a C- in grade 5 math. It may have been the pressure of my upcoming application to secondary school, or maybe it was a result of an unfilled knowledge gap. Either way, my teacher was not pleased. She labeled me as the lazy kid who ruined the class average. She lost confidence in me and no longer gave me opportunities to grow. I lost my momentum and fell into the *no one cares* pool in school from that point forward.

After feeling defeated, I received what I now know was a lucky break. I moved from Hong Kong to Canada when I was 16. Hong Kong, although a powerful financial hub in Asia, is still a small city of 7 million people and barely a dot on the world map. Canada suddenly made my world bigger, brighter, and full of opportunity. My first year in the foreign land was quite a challenge: not only did I have to translate every conversation from English to Chinese in my head, but I also had to find the courage to speak English to people who would immediately pick up on my accent. I was afraid people instantly knew I was "fresh off the boat" and would judge me. Because the curriculum in Hong Kong was so advanced, math in Canada was easy for me. Adapting to the new culture wasn't as bad as I'd thought. I was good at math, and I could use that leverage to make friends. Even more exciting, I could trade these skills with others who could help me with my English.

Redirected Energies and Refocusing My Life

The summer I turned 17 was a pivotal point in my life; it was one of the best and worst summers. I fell in love for the very first time with someone incredibly smart. I adored him. I wanted to be good enough for him and that desire turned into motivation in every aspect of my life. I became the best version of who I could be; all my time dedicated to academics and extracurricular activities showed. I reached the top of my class and won a few competitions. I saw a change in myself because I felt purpose in everything I did; it wasn't about the awards and achievements. Everything I saw became clearer and more beautiful.

I found a power and drive within me that I did not even know I had. I realized, for the first time, that I could be so much more and so much better than the past versions of myself. When I practiced a piano piece, I was able to connect in a deep, meaningful way to the composer's frame of mind when the piece was written. At my swimming competitions, I found a power of explosion, and felt as though I could be faster and better than others; I wanted to prove to myself that I deserved to be there. The day he abruptly dumped me, though, all I remember feeling was broken and devastated. I skipped school for weeks. I did not understand what I did wrong. In those dark moments, I found myself standing on the apartment's rooftop, contemplating jumping off the building. Still, the realization hit when I thought about how devastating it would be for my family. I decided to redirect the courage I was building to jump into building my best life.

I channeled all the energy from my broken heart into preparing for college. I shifted my focus to living my life and creating opportunities for myself. I trained myself like I was in the military. I became very competitive, and I did exceptionally well in competitions. I woke up early every morning to read the newspaper, practicing verbal English for an hour. I gave it my best in piano and swim practice. I sought out any opportunity I could to volunteer and worked 2 part-time jobs, teaching piano and tutoring math. Occasionally, I even played piano for wedding parties or babysat for extra money. I had many lonely and defeated moments that interfered with my focus. I sometimes felt sorry for myself and constantly had to slap myself and remind myself that I could not control what had happened, and that I did not need to justify my choices or mistakes. If I ever wanted someone to love me, I needed to learn to love myself first. Dedicating my energy and focus to building my best life was the only way I knew how to love myself at the time. Of course, deep down, I still missed the boy who broke my heart, but I never let it break my focus on the future. Maybe a small part of me hoped that perhaps one day he would see me shine and regret the mistake he made.

College Graduate in Denial

I always knew education would be the key to financial freedom and independence, so when I finally made it to college, I was thrilled. Unfortunately, another roadblock presented itself just when things were starting to look up again. I attended college in Toronto, a massive change from the super-small town in Canada I lived in until then. It was an eye-opening experience for me. The world was so much bigger than I had imagined, filled with talent from every corner. In a strange way, the wide range of people made me feel like I belonged for the first time in my life. Everywhere I looked, I saw someone different. We all had different strengths and backgrounds to bring to the table, especially when learning and working together on class projects or social clubs! I found my small group of people that could geek out with me on different topics, and I learned so much from the new perspectives and viewpoints! I often think of that environment as a bowl of the most nutritious soup—full of unique ingredients.

Deciding what to do after college was a struggle for me. The year I graduated coincided with the SARS outbreak in Hong Kong, making the job market ultracompetitive for new graduates. I had the option to stay in Canada or try my luck in the United States. Each choice felt more terrifying than the last. I was scared of entering the real world and taking on real responsibility.

The unconstrained period after college was supposed to feel invigorating, but I struggled to make a decision. I considered applying to law school, remembering how much I enjoyed analyzing cases in my business law classes. I really did not want to add more to the mountain of student loan debt I acquired, nor did I want to invest any more time into my education. Still, when I imagined how my life might look in 30 years' time, I felt terrified. Secure a job in the top public accounting firm, stack up a few promotions, earn good money, get married, have kids, a big house and dog, go on fancy vacations...and then what? Why was I discouraged by a life like this? Isn't that the dream? I didn't understand the purpose of my life, nor could I find the answers myself. Finally, I narrowed my choices down to 2 options: go with my then-boyfriend back to Hong Kong or stay in Canada. Although I didn't know much about my future, I did know I wanted more for myself than to be a shadow for a boy. Trusting my gut, I made the tough decision to stay in Canada.

CPA and Big 4...and Then What?

My degree was in finance and economics, so I thought a CPA credential would be a powerful addition to my toolkit. I must have sent more than 100 resumes and talked my way through endless interviews; finally, a mutual fund company in Boston offered me a position. Financial services always interested me, mainly because it's been a booming industry. Plus, it's impressive to work amongst all the smart people on Wall Street. The bank evolved in regulations to offer more financial products—not just deposits, but investment and insurance products. After 18 months of financial services experiences, I knew I needed more than just a stable job—I needed inspiration, excitement, and the kind of fulfillment that comes from overcoming big challenges. In 2005, I quit the job and moved back home to Hong Kong. It was time to see the rise of China that everyone was talking about.

I spent the next 3 years working as an auditor for 2 of the "Big 4" accounting firms in Hong Kong and in New York. On my first day as an auditor, I remember going into the headquarters wearing a suit, feeling proud. Ever since China joined the World Trade Organization (WTO) in 2001, many China-based private enterprises started going public via an IPO in the Hong Kong Stock Exchange. China's 4 big state-run banks, along with many other smaller banks, went public in 2005 and 2006, making it one of the best years in decades.

I was assigned to one of the most promising and fast-growing groups: the China market group. This involved intense travel to China. My first audit assignment was doing an IPO readiness audit evaluation and due diligence for a renowned electronic manufacturing client. It could not have been a more complex first assignment. Back in the early 2000s, many documents were in paper form. Most of my 12–18 hours a day were in the factory doing manual work—photocopying, marking up contracts and supporting documents, documenting every step, communicating to client teams, and learning simplified Chinese as I went. I started to get homesick with all the intense travel and factory stay, but I stuck it out and told myself to finish what I started: finish this project, then decide my next move. I knew that as a junior person, nothing was glamorous except for my suit and my BlackBerry (at the time!). I would have to complete a lot of grunt work in order to build the career I dreamed of. The boring tasks would serve as a way to learn and accumulate experiences to build a strong foundation in the early stages of my career. Even if I had gone to another company, or had taken a different job, the path would have been more or less the same in those early stages of my career. I could not quite see or understand the big picture at the time, but I knew, at the very least, that everything I did would help prepare me for my next move. I am glad that I stuck it out, because for the past decade, even as lots has changed in the way we do things, many of the fundamentals, concepts, and experiences continue to be reinforced. The grunt work made me a better professional and executive, as I am now able to connect everything all together to serve my clients. Our experiences never go to waste if we use them to serve us.

Big Apple, Big Company Culture, and the Many Hidden Ugly Politics

The year I spent in China was an eye-opening experience with great exposures, but I was ready to move back to North America. The alternative investment industry was booming in 2006, and I moved to New York to join another Big 4 accounting firm. Working for hedge funds and private equity companies provided a lot of perks and I wanted to be in the middle of the action.

My first client was a small startup hedge fund going through a first-time audit. In financial services, there are a lot of big personalities to deal with. I obviously did not have the skills to know how to deal with them, and I would often laugh off some ridiculous remarks. Most clients would want us to be on site just to show that we were working. I always thought that my results should be the only measurement of the quality of my work. Measuring commitment or skill on the time spent in the office felt like a lack of trust, but I toughed it out, knowing that my dedication would serve my ultimate goal of having a career I was proud of.

Working in a big company has a lot of advantages; it provided me with some incredible resources to learn and grow. Exposure to different clients is invaluable during the foundational years of any career. Eventually, that familiar feeling returned: I could no longer see myself committing to a long-term career in auditing. So, I left. After a full year of interviewing and careful consideration of all my options, I was recruited by an investment bank. It was an easy decision to work for a growing company, under a manager that valued my work and had my back. Yes! This was it. The first day I stepped foot in the group, I felt an unfamiliar electricity. It was intense and thrilling.

And then, it happened. By 2008, the entire world started to feel the upheaval of the biggest financial crisis in modern history. New announcements about changes and restructuring in the company poured out, including one about the firing of my direct boss. I felt like an orphan at work; there was no one there who supported me. I had to fight for myself.

As months of bad news dragged on, the mounting fear really brought out the worst in people. Colleagues regularly stole my work and took credit. I hated corporate politics, and I didn't know what to do. One day, in desperation, I walked the aisles of Barnes & Noble, searching for books to teach me how to play the corporate game. I couldn't do what was asked of me. I couldn't be nasty or more aggressive, or compromise myself just to fit in with the corporate culture of the time. Dealing with the toxic environment and negative culture was mentally exhausting. The energy that once fueled me, drained me. On top of everything else, I was doing the jobs of 2 or 3 people because layoffs left us constantly understaffed. The signs were obvious: it was time to find something new. I was mentally and physically exhausted and burned out. I needed a break. I wanted to go home.

The Need to Return Home

The following few months were spent regrouping in my parents' 600-square-foot apartment in Hong Kong. Thankfully, the US economy looked so bad that everyone agreed that I made the right choice of going home. My resume looked strong and I interviewed with a few impressive companies, but I couldn't manage to secure second-round interviews, much less a job offer. The hiring managers' and recruiters' feedback was consistent—they sensed that I didn't really want to be there. I told myself I needed to step up my game, prepare more, and act more enthusiastic. I practiced every detail: my answers, how to show my eagerness for the job—I even practiced showing a more genuine smile. Nothing was working. Without a job, I felt useless and lost. Something inside of me had gone missing.

I stitched together the money I needed for my mortgage and student loan payments through random teaching jobs in English and music, sometimes filling in for administrative tasks. Things went dark for a while. No matter how many temporary jobs I worked, I felt my vision and joy for life slipping away.

I always envisioned myself settling down in my 30s. My kids would be in school, and I'd take calls from my office on top of the corporate ladder. All the markers of a life on the right track. Instead, I found myself looking up from rock bottom, wondering if I'd already reached my peak. After a few months of being in a drug-addicted, tear-ridden slump, it was time to finally face *me*. The reflection was unrecognizable. The puffy eyes, tired skin, and a deep sense of sadness and despair...this couldn't be the person I turned out to be. I wanted to rewind to the happiest time and undo every bad thing that happened since. I missed New York and the feeling of accomplishment it gave me. I felt ashamed of myself, ashamed of letting anyone down. I threw away my career for this slump. Once again, I was down, but not out. It was time to rebuild.

Rebuilding through Differences

Starting over was incredibly hard! It took 6 months for me to find the courage to move back to New York and start building my life again; while it was happening, it felt like a million years. I was fortunate enough to have friends that let me crash on their couches while I found a corporate job again. I lived out of a suitcase for the next few months. Transitioning back to a full-time corporate job was hard, but what was even more difficult was transitioning back to a life I could be proud of. The very fact that you're reading this book proves that it all ended up working out.

I am very proud of how far I have come. Not everyone is granted the opportunity to work in major cities in Asia, North America, and Europe. Not only did I experience all of life's highs and lows in those areas, but I also learned to embrace the best of each region. Even though I may still carry a "watered down" accent or a few painful memories, living across many cities in the past few decades has taught me the strength and power of embracing each other's differences and uniqueness, utilizing diversity to encourage creativity and strategic thinking in accounting and finance.

Being different, after all, is actually pretty cool! And, being able to bring these differences into my work made my career more interesting!

Hopefully this book serves as the culmination of the best advice and most interesting stories from as many different perspectives as possible for you to use in your upcoming journey. Navigating the world of accounting and its many options can be challenging, confusing, and frustrating. Having trusted mentors, and being able to seek insider advice from professionals who have walked the path, is often tremendously valuable. To help you feel connected with the accounting world and some of its most impressive members, this book features 20 stories of selected thought leaders in their respective fields, giving you insights into 20 amazing mentors. My hope is that reading this book will give you a greater understanding of what accountants do, all while you gain substantial insights, perspectives, guidance, and inspiration from each of these unique stories.

The world is so big, and its opportunities are beyond your imagination. No one was around to tell that to my younger self, so I'm taking the opportunity to tell you now. The world keeps changing: what you know or want today may be totally different a year from now. If you keep building skills, experiences, and knowledge, though, no one can take that away from you. Meanwhile, enjoy the ride, have a lot of fun exploring and experiencing different things, and allow your journey to unfold.

It is an incredible honor to have you join me and the amazing mentors featured in this book on this exploratory ride!

Forensic Accounting And Investigations

Fraud and scammers are everywhere. They often infiltrate accountants' work, targeting vulnerabilities as a way to attain personal wealth. Forensic accountants are the ones who work relentlessly to catch the bad guys with their investigative and auditing techniques. Part of forensic accounting often includes testifying in court as an expert witness against fraud and scammers. If forensic accounting is your passion, expect to be highly regarded and valuable in almost every industry, including financial services firms, banks, police forces, government agencies, and the Federal Bureau of Investigation (FBI). Expect to work on a variety of assignments like investigating financial crimes or hidden assets (in custody and divorce settlement cases), establishing damages from insurance claims, or evaluating businesses on the basis of their finances.

Throughout the 1980s, the accounting and auditing industry was self-regulated. Accounting firms were confident in their ability to maintain their independence and their relationships with their clients. Conflict-of-interest requirements and laws did not exist. Although all seemed to be progressing perfectly, many corporate accounting scandals and fraud cases of the early 2000s came to light. The Enron, WorldCom, AIG bailout, Lehman Brothers, and Madoff investment scandals are just some of the better-known fraud cases. With the increase of fraudulent scandals came a greater tightening of our financial system with complex and ever-changing regulations. Only then did this particular field gain the recognition and attention it deserved from the public.

In 1987, Dr. Joseph Wells changed the world of forensic accounting by introducing the idea of a white-collar accountant. He began the ACFE (Association of Certified Fraud Examiners) in 1988 with the idea that organizations should promote a stellar tone at the top, not just in word but also in deed. Top management, he argued, needed to set the tone; their message would then affect the ethics and performances of their employees. Today, the ACFE organization offers training and certification programs (CFE-Certified Fraud Examiner) for aspiring and experienced fraud professionals throughout the world.

The financial systems of the United States are complex and ever-changing. Greed for money will always be the root cause of financial crime. The demand for highly skilled forensic accountants will continue to grow. Luckily, forensic accountants work everywhere. Companies of all sizes hire forensic accountants to investigate any suspicious activities of internal fraud such as embezzlement. Acting similar to private investigators, forensic accountants train in specialized skills such as auditing, investigating, and interviewing. With their experiences, most of the time they are able to uncover suspicious activity, which you and I may not see right away!

To help you understand if forensic accounting is the right choice for you, I talked to Tom Golden, Isabel Mercedes Cumming, and Tony Menendez. These 3 are relentless in their pursuit of the truth. Although unique in their philosophies, each has the experience, skills, character, and intuition to detect things that others may not see right away.

If you are someone who values curiosity, moral courage, and holding people accountable even when it's hard, and enjoy getting to the bottom of these issues, take the time to hear what Tom, Isabel, and Tony have to say to be the best in the field! You may be the perfect person to join this noble field!

2

Cigarette Salesman Turned Big 4 Forensic Accounting Partner, and Fiction Author

Tom Golden

RETIRED PARTNER AT PRICEWATERHOUSECOOPERS, AUTHOR, AND SPEAKER

WWW.TOMGOLDENBOOKS.COM

I first met Tom through his accounting fraud thriller novel Sunday Night Fears*—the first in a series of fictionalized accounts of Tom's career in forensic accounting investigation. As Tom says, "Forensic accountants are the Navy SEALs of the accounting industry." Over the course of Tom's*

career, his investigations have been exciting and intense, providing more than enough inspiration for multiple novels.

Talking to Tom is like having a front-row seat to the evolution of the audit and forensic accounting industry. His career journey evolution, which began in 1982, is remarkable. It also brings the promise that accounting careers and responsibilities will continue to expand and grow in the ever-changing industry. His management philosophy brings out the best in people, as evidenced in the successful practice he built over the years. If his career resonates with you, I encourage you to pay close attention to his persistence and strong ethics. It's part of what has made him so revered in the industry.

Since retiring from PricewaterhouseCoopers (PwC), Tom continues to engage in all that he enjoys and does best. He speaks at events, writes, and conducts high-profile investigations. He still mentors aspiring accounting professionals from around the world. I am hoping to see his novels developed into a financial thriller movie or television drama. There are so many TV dramas that portray the medical corridors, the courtrooms of the legal world, and the flashy businesses of Silicon Valley. It's about time accounting thrillers made their debut!

Atypical Path

I was born in Pittsburgh, Pennsylvania, and grew up in Philadelphia and Central Jersey. It was tough growing up with an alcoholic father who had frequent angry outbursts and derided me at every turn. I ground through those days, eventually graduating high school and enrolling in an out-of-state college to get away from him. While there, I was fortunate to meet the love of my life and marry her at age 20.

My wife changed my outlook on failure, growth, and the possibilities of the world. I always thought I would grow up to be an English teacher like my mother, but the girl I would eventually marry told me I didn't look like an English major—whatever that meant—so I changed my major to marketing and started down a winding career path. After college, I exited the job search with a position as a sales representative for the RJ Reynolds Tobacco Company, moved to Indianapolis, Indiana, and spent the next 9 years selling cigarettes out of the trunk of my car.

In 1979, however, I felt new inspiration to improve my career and myself. I read an article in *The Wall Street Journal* that explained how the Big 8 accounting firms wanted to add consulting to their traditional audit and tax lines. The article proceeded to mock the industry as full of geeks who couldn't sell. I knew I was a great salesman and contemplated how I could position myself to join one of the Big 8 firms. It never occurred to me that I was not an accountant! I mean... who does that?

I met with an HR director at one of the Big 8 firms who showed me a pathway while mentioning that it would be crazy to attempt a new career in accounting at my age. Undeterred, I presented the idea to my wife. With her encouragement, I started down an entirely new career path, and 2 years later I had earned an MBA from Indiana University and passed 3 parts of the CPA exam on my first sitting. I failed the auditing exam...the one skill critical to joining an audit firm! Still, I talked my way into landing an associate audit position at Coopers & Lybrand (C&L), one of the merged firms of PwC. I was the oldest person they ever hired for that position in the history of the Indianapolis office—fully a decade older than my colleagues. As I said, I was a good salesman.

The Oldest and Least Experienced Enters the Room...and Shakes Things Up

My colleagues called my hiring "an experiment." They ostracized me in more ways than one, but I was determined to prove my worth and make a difference at the firm. Over the next 18 months, I was assigned to jobs no one else wanted to do: pension audits, inventory assignments, and out-of-town busywork. No one would take me on an audit engagement, likely thinking I wouldn't be around much longer. It was frustrating, but I knew all I needed was an opportunity.

And then someone took a chance on me. I was assigned to my first public company audit. It was a leasing company, and I was tasked to audit the largest asset on the balance sheet—lease contracts receivable. Something seemed off 2 weeks in, but I couldn't summon the courage to say anything to my supervisor. Heck, I had failed the auditing portion of the CPA exam and never had a class in auditing! I had no credibility. What I did have, though, was innate distrust.

My relationship with my dad created a sense that things are likely not as they seem. In my opinion, the signatures on the leasing documents were suspicious. I didn't trust them, or the lease approval and entry process. Something didn't add up, but I needed more evidence to prove fraud before I would risk bringing it to the attention of the higher-ups.

Soon, I came to a stopping point, realizing I had neither the accounting and auditing skills nor an intimate knowledge of the company I was auditing. I had to find *One Honest Soul* (the inspiration and title of the second book in my novel series) at the leasing company that could help me get to the bottom of it all. Someone who knew the company inside and out and could help me navigate uncharted waters. Utilizing my people skills mastered as a salesman, I found her. The one person who was looking for someone to help her do the right thing. Together, we compiled all of the evidence of the accounting fraud I had discovered. But that was only half the task. I still needed help linking the facts with the applicable accounting and regulatory rules.

Over the Christmas break, I reached out to a friend, an MBA class-mate of mine, who then worked as a controller in another public com-pany. I asked him to guide me in navigating the regulatory waters. We sat and walked through all the company's previous SEC filings and current financial statements. By the end of the holiday season, I had a comprehensive list of questions to resolve when I returned for the year-end fieldwork. About 2 weeks later, while nearing completion of the audit, I became more convinced the company officers were running a massive leasing scam and I decided to speak up.

Finally, just 5 days until the company's earnings release date, I found a new resolve. Still working at the company site at 2 o'clock in the morn-ing, I picked up the phone to report what I had discovered—not to my supervisor, but to the engagement partner. I called him at home and pleaded for him to review my evidence package. Reluctantly, he agreed to review the evidence I had assembled. He arrived an hour later, took my evidence package, and shut himself in an office to review what I found.

I sat outside, pensive, wondering if I had made a huge mistake. I imagined I'd be fired on the spot. To my amazement, he emerged an hour later, looked at me, and said, "We have a big problem. I think you have uncovered a leasing fraud. I need to notify the board of directors immediately." Several hours later, I was standing in front of the board, explaining what I had discovered.

When the board delayed its earnings release, the company's stock dropped from $33 to $8 per share in a single hour, and trading was suspended. Over the next year, I spent countless hours being inter-viewed by SEC Enforcement and the FBI as their lead witness in their investigations against the company, its officers and directors, and my own firm. The firm hired outside counsel to work with me on how to testify and conduct a further investigation. We learned the fraud extended to previous years but escaped detection by other auditors. Those same ones who mocked my hiring.

Several of the firm's thought leaders realized some remediation was necessary in light of my discovery—not related to the procedures employed, but rather to the mindset of the auditor while in the performance of their duties. The firm produced a short video of me presenting my approach to professional skepticism and showed it around the country.

In 1991 I was granted the opportunity to start the office's first consulting practice, the whole reason that the forward-thinking managing partner agreed to take a chance on me 9 years earlier. In 4 short years, my forensic accounting practice was generating a third of the gross margin of the entire Indianapolis office, at only 10 percent of the cost. I became a partner in 1996 and was immediately transferred to Chicago to establish and grow a forensic accounting practice there. Upon retiring in 2008, my Chicago practice was the second-largest practice in the US firm of PwC.

Share the Credit, Succeed Together

While I have given hundreds of speeches on the art of financial crime investigation, what many find most interesting is how I found success in a competitive industry without the customary education and experience. Sure, I had a lot of people helping me along the way, but if asked what skill was most responsible for my success, the answer might surprise many. My ability to persuade people to do what I wanted them to do has been most valuable in my career success. My ability to persuade clients to hire me, recruits to come work for me, and the best of those professionals to trust me with their careers, I owe to the wisdom of Dale Carnegie.

The lessons to take away from my incredibly successful journey at PwC are embedded in Dale Carnegie's rules for working with others, the importance of seeking and accepting honest feedback, and personal determination in overcoming obstacles most of us face: fear, anxiety, and rejection. I knew in my heart what I wanted to do, and every day I tried my hardest to reach my goals.

Some takeaways for you? Get a mentor outside of the organization where you work. Read *How to Win Friends and Influence People* by Dale Carnegie and practice his suggestions often. Set your sights on goals and establish strategies to achieve them. Be aggressive in those goals and know that if you are not failing from time to time, you are not challenging yourself (more on that in a moment). The world is waiting, no matter how old you are!

Mastering the Art of Human Relations

At PwC, we were fortunate to hire the best and the brightest from the best schools. If a colleague in my practice would tell me they were smart and hardworking, I'd respond that they were like 95 percent of everyone at the firm. "Tell me how you are different in a way that can make a difference," I would often say. Of course, I showed them how: *to win over thy fellow human being...learn what they want...and give it to them.* That is the secret to achieving anything you want.

One of my marketing professors taught me that lesson when I was just 18. He gave me a copy of *How to Win Friends and Influence People.* I quickly tapped into its special powers and, over the years, found it to be the most effective resource available for mastering the art of human relations. At the heart of it all is simply to think about what you want, then flip it around and give it to others. Do it sincerely and consistently, and before long, you'll be amazed at how quickly people will give you what you want.

Among his many techniques, Carnegie teaches you to be lavish in your praise and share credit freely and often. Let me share a story that may shed some light on how influential Dale Carnegie's book can be in your success.

In the middle of my career, John Wiley & Sons (Wiley), the largest business book publisher in the world, reached out to me to write a book that they would market globally as "the seminal guide to forensic accounting investigation." I quickly found PwC was excited about the project and approved it, but I knew I could not complete such a massive undertaking alone. I mean, this was "the seminal guide." There were some areas of financial crime investigation I believed I was an expert at doing, such as planning and performing an investigation, interview and interrogation, and testifying. But in many others, I knew I was not a qualified expert. There were others who knew much more about data mining technology, the Foreign Corrupt Practices Act (FCPA), and many others. The firm had such experts, but they didn't work for me. They also were partners. How could I get them to take on such a project considering they had very busy lives?

PwC told me to "work out the details," and I signed a contract with Wiley to produce and edit the book and purchase 30,000 copies to distribute globally to partners, staff, and clients. Fortunately, PwC, and not I, footed the bill for that! I immediately set upon identifying the best of the firm's partners and staff worldwide to write the expert advice contained in that over-500-page book.

At the time, I was just a line partner with no authority to "assign" other partners to help me in this massive project ultimately taking over

3 years to write, edit, and publish. Yet, I convinced over 40 partners and staff from around the world to author and edit chapters. How was I able to do that?

Simple. Following Dale Carnegie's advice, I was lavish in my praise and shared the credit freely and often. Keep in mind this was my book. Only PwC and I signed the contract with Wiley. One would expect my name to appear on the book cover. Well, it did, but that cover also bears the names of 2 others, recognizing their significant contributions in editing the entire book—a task that took nearly a year to complete. There are even some chapters that I rewrote but bear another's sole name because those authors generously spent their time compiling the information. I did not care who received the credit. *A Guide to Forensic Accounting Investigation*, now in its second edition, was a huge success, even winning a publisher's award. Thank you, Dale Carnegie!

Without Dale Carnegie's sage advice, there was no way I'd have even been hired at the age of 32, with no CPA certification and only 9 hours in accounting course credits, let alone achieve all that I had. This is why I gave a copy of *How to Win Friends and Influence People* to each of my staff, requiring them to read and practice it daily. I still mentor accounting professionals around the globe, and heartily recommend this book. First published in 1936 and updated throughout the years, Dale Carnegie's masterpiece has timeless advice waiting for you.

Learning through Failure

I have been coaching and mentoring others for over 35 years. There is one immutable fact: people who refuse to leave their comfort zones early in their careers, and do so often, miss their best opportunities for learning and growth. You only remember the questions you got wrong on the test, the ones you *failed* to answer correctly.

It's human nature to avoid tasks where the opportunity for failure is high, but those are golden nugget learning opportunities! Don't pass them up. I'd encourage you to seek them out.

During the interview process for new recruits, I had my staff show me candidates they felt would succeed. Of course, they knew what I was seeking. I didn't want those kids who spent their youth bubble-wrapped from failure. I was the final interviewer in the hiring process, and I made it a point to tell every candidate that they would learn through criticism and failure. If hired, I would continually watch their progress and look for opportunities to stretch them, knowing that only then would they grow into the competent business professionals I expected them to become. And I would test them early and often.

One of my new hires, Jennifer, joined our office out of a top school, ready to work hard and move up to become a partner one day. The first task I gave her was to plan a Friday happy hour for our group. But she was new. What if she screwed it up? It's just a happy hour! Still, it was an opportunity for learning with no risk to the practice.

I asked her to get us a private room, consult with the other staff on how others had planned them in the past, and schedule it for the coming Friday. Her first week on the job, she was mingling with her coworkers and supervisors, getting to know them, asking how things were normally done around here, and working through the logistics of the event she was in charge of planning.

On the day of the event, we walked into the bar, but our private room was filled with other people. Jennifer checked with the bar staff and came back to me in tears, "They screwed it up and lost our reservation. It's not my fault!" I asked, "Jennifer, when did you confirm it?" Blank stare. As I thought, she had made a classic mistake. She *assumed* without checking with the bar to *ensure* they had the reservation. I told everyone I was headed home and wished all a good weekend. I ignored

Jennifer and left. I knew the staff would comfort her and tell her all the things she did wrong and what she needed to do first thing Monday morning. The learning process had begun.

When I got to my office on Monday morning, Jennifer was waiting for me with a notepad, pen, and apologies. She promised that a mix-up like that wouldn't happen again. I said, "Of course it won't. You'll plan this week's happy hour, too!" I knew she would not waste the opportunity for a do-over. Everyone in the office was cheering her on, but leaving her to plan it on her own.

So, how did it turn out? Let's just say that nearly 20 years later, when some of us get together and reminisce, we recall that happy hour as the best ever! Jennifer learned some valuable lessons that would help her be successful at the firm and in life. Of course, the challenges I offered my staff were thoughtfully timed in keeping with one's experience and capabilities. Although they may not have realized it, I always knew what they were capable of at any given time.

Having a willingness for your team to fail comes with comfort in ceding control—a difficult task for many leaders. Ronald Reagan had a philosophy I try to practice often. He said, "Surround yourself with the most intelligent people you can find, delegate authority, and don't interfere." Of course, considering the high-risk nature of what we did—criminal investigations—I stayed just close enough to ensure mistakes were caught timely and rectified, ensuring positive outcomes. I always believed that trust and ownership brought out the best in everyone in my practice.

Here's a tip for keeping your best people motivated. Don't micromanage them. Especially your best people. See them as your future partners. If you're paying attention, you'll spot them early enough. Watch them closely. Give them the best opportunities. Some might say that's not fair. That everyone should share in those opportunities. And to an extent they are correct. All of our employees are important, but *some* are more important than others. If you treat *all* your employees equally, you will lose your best people. Our greatest asset, our people, go down the elevator every night. We need to make sure we motivate our best people to come back up the elevator in the morning.

A word on criticism: it should be given often and as close to the event as possible. I would tell my staff that if they were not making mistakes here and there, then they were not being assigned challenging tasks. Expect to make mistakes. Expect to be criticized. It's part of growing and learning. I also found the best way to criticize, especially on the big failures, maybe ones that resulted in an angry client, was to look back to when I had made a similar mistake. Lord knows that I've made plenty of them! My staff sees me as successful; they need to realize I've made similar mistakes. Suddenly, it doesn't seem so bad to them. It's all part of the learning experience.

If you are a staff person reading this, and you too want to learn and grow, do this. Give your supervisors permission to criticize you. Most of them don't like to criticize. So, they put it off until months after the engagement ended, and they are just getting around to completing your evaluation. Instead, try this on your next assignment.

"Bob, I just learned that I will be working with you on the Hampton audit next week. I hope I will do most tasks correctly, but I'm sure I will make some mistakes. Please tell me where I mess up as close to the event as possible. You'd be doing me a big favor. Thanks!" You will find that little offer will be met with supervisors now wanting to make you the best that you can be. Those supervisors will be among your heartiest supporters throughout your career. Try it. You'll be glad you did.

In the end, I want to impart one more suggestion. Never, never, ever give up on your dreams. Imagine way back in 1979 if I had not decided to take a chance on achieving my impossible dream. Where would I be today? Hard to say, but I can tell you this: I'm sure glad I bet on myself. I'm pretty happy with how it all turned out.

Leave your comfort zone as much as possible. You will never see the best version of yourself until you do.

3

The People's Investigator
Solving Cases like Nancy Drew

Isabel Mercedes Cumming

ATTORNEY, INSPECTOR GENERAL
OF BALTIMORE CITY

Isabel is a fireball of energy. She is intimidating not only by virtue of being an attorney and accountant representing the citizens in Baltimore but also because she is fiercely intelligent and sharply analytical. She reminds me of Dana Scully, the fictional FBI agent and medical doctor in The X-Files, *or Captain Olivia Benson of* Law & Order: Special Victims Unit. *Like these fictional heroic characters, she stops at nothing to find out the truth and keep society in order.*

Although rising up in the male-dominated political world as a female is hard, Isabel is incredibly accomplished. Part of her success comes from her refreshing, authentic, and honest way of speaking. She always says it like it is. We don't see enough of that from professionals who work in the political world. It can be tempting to believe that the only way to get into politics is through connections. Isabel, however, stands out as an example of how to reach a powerful position by simply having a strong work ethic and values. She uses her power and knowledge to make the world more just.

Isabel continually proved herself as a leader and an asset in all of her positions, the latest of which is in Baltimore City. I am excited to see what will come from this incredible accountant and attorney. My hope is that Isabel's story will inspire newfound confidence in readers to not only pursue a career in accounting, law enforcement, and politics, but also to have the courage and strength to stand up and speak up for themselves, for causes that they believe in, and for the people they care about.

Anything but the "Virgin Vault"

When I enrolled at James Madison University to major in political science, I had no idea how my love of solving mysteries would serve me in my future career. I knew first that I had to get my living situation straightened out, which required a little detective work along with some thinking on my feet.

My parents intended for me to stay in the "Virgin Vault," a no-alcohol, no-visitations-from-the-opposite-gender dormitory. Lucky for me, though, those dorms were overcrowded, and I was temporarily placed in a 5-day visitation dorm for the upper-class students. When I moved in, I learned the Student Government Association (SGA) senator could not be moved out. I'd never run for office in my life, but I knew that I wanted to stay in that dorm, not the "Virgin Vault," so I decided to run for SGA senator. The dorm mother told me that there was no way I would win against the incumbent.

After I figured out what the word incumbent meant, I began canvassing all the residents around the dormitory, telling everyone about my parents' plan and promising how hard I would work for them. It worked, and I became a senator of an upperclassman dorm as a freshman, an achievement that was unheard of. Most importantly, I was able to stay in that dorm. As I reported to the legislative president for my first day as an SGA senator, I learned that I needed to join a committee. He recommended the food services committee; it was the most popular committee because "everyone eats." At that moment, 2 upperclassmen came bursting into the room. One was the president of the Interfraternity Council and the other was the head of the dining hall. They kept cursing and arguing, making a verbal mess of the SGA Office. The legislative vice president cut in, shut them both up, and said he was giving the chairmanship to "the freshman." I remember standing there, shocked, nervous, and also excited! I knew nothing about food services except that my mother raised us not to waste our food.

So, I started with what I knew. Whether in politics, accounting, or law, it turns out that having the right mindset and principles is as important as expertise. I didn't know much about the topic, but I knew how to gather data and use it to improve students' experiences. I developed a physical food waste survey, pulling the "finished trays" and going through the actual food waste to determine how much students wasted on their plates by evaluating how much they threw away. It was a dirty, disgusting job, but with that raw data, I was able to institute a second policy that saved the students a quarter of a million dollars in tuition. The savings to the students and my role in instituting that policy earned me the Senator of the Year award. It was the first time in history that a freshman had ever won the award. It wasn't that I was an expert. I had learned how to logically and analytically look at a problem, starting with what I knew.

By my senior year, I was elected student government president and spoke at my own convocation in front of 25,000 people, the first student to speak in over 25 years. All of this experience helped me when it came to applying for jobs. There weren't many accounting majors involved in student government, so I stood out. When I graduated, I had a lot of offers, all from the Big 8 accounting firms.

In the Footsteps of Nancy Drew

When I was a little girl, the Nancy Drew books were my favorites. I loved piecing together the clues and solving the mystery along with Nancy. I like to think that's what I do now in many ways. I just wanted to find the truth in everything, using all my skills.

I came from a mixed background—my Canadian father and Puerto Rican mother instilled in me the value of serving and giving back to the community that shaped who I have become. To me, that is the Hispanic community. In everything I do, I hope that I change someone's life for the better.

In every step of my career, there was a hint of where I would go next. In college, I studied accounting and helped the student body save a lot of money. I loved helping people, and I knew I could do that with my skill in numbers. So, then I became an accountant, a lawyer, a fraud specialist, and an inspector general.

When I was in law school, I had the opportunity to work in juvenile justice. In some ways, their crimes could be understood. Their stories were so sad; life handed them some difficult cards. But white-collar criminals are very different; they have the best of everything, and they think they're the smartest person in the room. It all comes down to greed. And the worst thing is...they could be the person sitting next to you!

My first accounting job was working as a savings loan specialist at KPMG in the midst of the savings and loan crisis, and I looked for fraud in particular. After that, I went to work for American National Bank, as director of internal audit, again with fraud as my focus. I realized my accounting background made it so much easier for me to crack fraud cases. The work was intense and demanding, and I loved it.

I got such a thrill from solving fraud cases that I decided to go to school at night to first get an MBA, and then a law degree, while working full-time. For 3 years straight, I applied for an unpaid internship with the US Attorney's Office. Predictably, without any helpful connections, I was turned down. Finally, after my third round of applications, I was selected. There were 5 young men, all from top schools. Me, from the night program of the University of Baltimore. But after that summer, I had my own office and was allowed to stay on for 7 more months working on large cases while they all went back to their prestigious schools. I landed a great position with the Maryland State Prosecutor and later I asked my boss why he hired me. He told me that he knew all of my references and loved my accounting background. So, without that sacrifice of 9 months without a paycheck to get *that* experience and *those* contacts, I wouldn't have had the career I've had.

Equipped with my undergraduate accounting degree, MBA, and a law degree, I became an assistant state prosecutor. I used my accounting skills to continue to look for fraud and prosecute white-collar criminals. Knowing how to do a balance sheet and understanding the way business is run has been the most valuable education in my career in politics and fraud investigation. For 7 years, I worked on several large corruption cases at the Maryland State Prosecutor's Office and then went to become an assistant state's attorney in the largest jurisdiction in Maryland—Baltimore City—to fine-tune my trial skills for 4 more years.

My next stop was as the head of economic crimes and police conduct at Prince George's County State's Attorney's Office (SAO), right outside of Washington, DC. We had the first mortgage fraud unit in the United States, plus an identity theft unit and an elder abuse unit. *The Washington Post* called my unit "The Shining Star" of my boss's administration. After that, I was named head of investigations for the Washington DC Metro (WMATA) Office of the Inspector General for 7 years.

Always Set Your Goals High, Because It Is Never Enough Just to Get By

I've built teams up from almost nothing. At DC Metro, I started the position with an agency of one. When I left 7 years later, there were 14. At Prince George's SAO, I grew the team from 2 attorneys to 14. In Baltimore City, my team has grown from 4 to 17. What makes me successful is that I hire very good people; I hire people that I trust and that I think are incredibly competent. Above all, I want a team with integrity.

It was very important to me that the office only hired people that had great people skills. More than that, I want professionals who believe in treating everyone with kindness. I have a secret signal with my executive assistant to let me know when someone comes into an interview and is rude in any way. It is an automatic disqualification. The chief executive officer is never going to give you the tip; it's always the janitor, the people on the ground, and the people who are working in the weeds who we look to for recommendations. The value of being kind transcends the necessity of our work, but it is an integral part of it.

Another thing that I do during the hiring process is ensure that I only hire people who really understand the value of the work itself. I never want to micromanage, so I need a team of people who work with accountability and a sense of responsibility. They will complete their tasks, likely above and beyond expectations, because they care, and because they can. My trust in others helped me to build effective teams in 3 different positions, grow departments to triple their original size, and keep on moving forward in my career. I found that setting my goals high inspired me to hire only the best, and my teams had endless, actionable results.

I did all of this because I saw how to apply skills from one position to another, and I had the tenacity to continue growing, no matter my job title. There is so much to gain from doing your job well. You might be able to get away with underachieving in your position, but you'll really get the most out of your time by doing a good job.

When you push yourself, then you can take what you learned in that position and move it to the next opportunity. If you constantly underachieve, you won't push the boundaries of what you already know, and you won't gain much from your time.

Mutual Respect and Support

All my life, I've worked primarily with men. I try hard to treat everyone with the utmost respect, and I won't put up with anyone's nonsense. If someone says something inappropriate, I will call them out in a way that leaves space for them to step up. I try to be fair. For women working in male-dominated fields, I think a mentor is an important resource to have, so I mentor a lot of women. I am often encouraged to see women supporting each other in the workplace or outside of work, and how most of them will pay it forward and help others. I'm sure a lot of people have helped you along the way, and it's the right thing to do to return the favor. I worked with some amazing female attorneys at the US Attorney's Office who became great role models for me. It also certainly feels great to say that I am the first woman ever to be named the Inspector General of Baltimore City.

You're Never Going to Be Good at Skateboarding If You Can't Get Back Up

When I look back, I tend to glaze over the tough times, but there have been many failures in my life, and from the failures, you learn. As my professional skateboarding son always says, "You're never going to be good at skateboarding if you can't get back up." I learned from him, as I have from my past experiences, the value of pushing through difficult times, getting back on 2 feet, and hitting the ground running.

I always dreamed of being the Maryland state prosecutor. When I applied for the position, everybody told me that the position was sure to be mine. Unfortunately, I fell off the metaphorical skateboard when I ended up being the runner-up. I would have been the first woman and the first Hispanic to occupy the seat. Devastated, I started over into the world of inspector generals in 2011 to work for the metro system in Washington, DC. The new position continued the 4-hour commute I had for 7 more years. In the end, I commuted almost 4 hours a day for 14 years.

There's nothing glamorous about commuting 4 hours a day. There's nothing easy about commuting 4 hours a day. I had 2 young kids. For many of those years, I was a single mom. Those were some pretty hard years, but they taught me the value of moving forward with your head held high. Whatever life deals you, you cannot stop, you cannot give up, and you cannot feel sorry for yourself because there are other people that have had it far worse. Although the commute was long, and the hours tiring, I held pride in all of my new positions and excitement about the future. Your mindset is the key to success.

Get back on the skateboard. You'll enjoy the ride.

Serving the People and City I Love, No Matter How Absurd the Cases May Be

I took a significant pay cut to become the inspector general of Baltimore City in 2018. I knew I could make a difference, and I really loved this city. I am honored to be the first woman in this position, and I am committed to doing the best job I can for everyone who places their trust in me. I want to make them proud! I go after fraud, financial waste, and abuse for the city. If someone receives funds, works for Baltimore, or is under a procurement type of contract with Baltimore, then I have the ability to investigate them and find out whether or not they are wasting our money, and if they're involved in any type of fraud situation.

When I took the position, I focused on building a strong team to serve the citizens of Baltimore. We started with just 4 agents in the office; we now have 17. At first, our office came out with 8 reports a year; this year, we've issued 47 reports and saved almost $3 million with it. The number of hotline calls has jumped as well, from 72 to 751.

Every case is different—you never know what's coming in on any given day. While my office has removed people in high roles, we've also saved people's jobs. We discovered an exclusive neighborhood that was getting their trash picked up twice a week, instead of the city-mandated once a week, like every other neighborhood. By investigating and stopping this treatment, we saved our citizens about $120,000. In another example, one of Baltimore's iconic skating rinks had a manager who decided that he would make money by renting the skating rink out and not reporting the money. He ended up being terminated. We had another case that involved the elected Comptroller of Baltimore, who had voted for the sale of property to benefit a church that she was a board member of.

One funny anecdote comes from complaints we received that someone put in for bereavement leave because their uncle had died. In reality, that wasn't true. She provided a fake obituary and even changed the date on it. It said the person died on February 30th. There is no February 30th—even in a leap year, our calendar doesn't have February 30th! It turned out, this person had taken the money and gone on a cruise, posting all about it on Facebook.

For another example, we can turn to one where I saved 2 people's jobs! There was an article in the newspaper about 2 employees who went on a big trip to South by Southwest, the music festival in Austin, Texas. The newspaper wrote it was a wasted trip and that these women spent too much money and stayed down there for 10 days. Both of their pictures were in the newspaper. My hotline that morning was full of calls to "fire these people, this is horrible, they should lose their jobs!" We ended up doing an investigation, and it turned out that what the newspaper said wasn't accurate. These employees ended up saving city dollars, were only there for 4 days, and it ended up being clearly the opposite of what the newspaper reported. We saved their jobs. Honestly, we are proudest of the work we have done for people whose jobs we have saved. More than that, I am humbled by the people who told me the OIG was their last chance, and we saved the situation. I'm proudest to represent the people of Baltimore City as their investigator.

The common denominator in all the cases that we investigate, uncover, and prosecute is greed. People think they can get away with things or even cut corners. This greed, which has been a theme permeated throughout my accounting and public roles, inspires me every day to constantly push forward to pursue justice.

4

The Whistleblower's Tale
Managerial Courage of the Smokey Bear

Tony Menendez

ACCOUNTING PROFESSOR, WHISTLEBLOWER
AT HALLIBURTON, AND FORMER EXECUTIVE
AT GENERAL MOTORS AND ERNST & YOUNG

*Tony is perhaps best known as the "accountant who beat Halliburton."
For his notable contributions to the profession, he has been honored
with the Accounting Exemplar Award from the American Accounting
Association and the Sentinel Award from the Association of Certified
Fraud Examiners. He is widely recognized for his decade-long legal battle
with Halliburton as a corporate whistleblower under the Sarbanes-Oxley*

Act (SOX). Although that's quite an accomplishment, Tony is so much more than that! Throughout his 25-year career, Tony reinvented himself 3 times and had 3 different career paths, all with dramatic twists and turns. Alongside solving complex technical accounting, reporting, and auditing issues as an external auditor, he has been a corporate controller and forensic accountant. Tony has tons of practical wisdom to share, and that he does. As a former top controller for General Motors (GM), he played an important role in GM's historic effort to emerge from bankruptcy and complete one of the largest IPOs in history. As a former audit executive with Ernst & Young (EY), he focused on entrepreneurial emerging growth companies involved in complex business transactions and companies navigating the IPO journey. As a litigation consultant, he has worked on numerous nationally litigated cases with attorneys representing individuals and shareholders in cases involving allegations of accounting malpractice and fraud. Today, he is the George A. Dasaro distinguished clinical assistant professor of accounting at Loyola Marymount University where he teaches financial accounting, auditing, and fraud examination courses, equipping the next generations of leaders with the necessary tools, skills, and mindsets to fight against accounting fraud and for the protection of the public interest.

Doing the right thing and standing by what you believe in is much harder than it appears to be, especially because it may often feel as though everything in the world is against you. Fighting against powerful corporations and executives is a lonely battle and one that really shakes your hopes and optimism. Some consider Tony an unsung hero, while others may call him crazy—thinking he should have just walked away from the fraud and quit.

I admire his persistence and courage; it takes irrational courage to be able to bust and fight for what we believe and know is right. We need more people like him to build a better world and society!

The Beginning of My Rollercoaster Ride

I've traveled down a winding road in my career, riding the roller coaster of successes, failures, mistakes, and courage in an ever-changing manner. I am often humbled when I remember what I have accomplished and the experiences and opportunities I have had that helped me grow personally and professionally into who I am today. As one of 11 children in my family, I grew up very modest. My jovial dad owned a small paving and construction company and had an eighth grade education. My mother was a lifelong learner who worked in administration at the University of Houston and, later in life, got her undergraduate and graduate degrees while supporting our family. It was during the summers, when my father made me work construction, that I learned what physical hard work was really about. He would always tell me that he wanted me to make a living because of what was in my head, instead of my muscles. My mom encouraged me to read, and during breaks from school, she would take me to the museums and the occasional archaeological dig site to excavate ancient Native American artifacts. Growing up, I never had any interest in going into business. My dad's struggling little business did little to glamorize the whole thing.

Instead, I was fascinated with baseball, dinosaurs, ancient civilizations, space, and science fiction. In college, when my dreams of becoming a professional baseball player came to an end, I considered a career as a geologist or a paleontologist. Science classes made me marvel at how big the world was. Now, I can see how this peculiar curiosity served me well when encountering suspicious issues. It was that same curiosity that drove me to dig deeper and uncover the truth.

In addition to my studies, I had a part-time job as a waiter at a local Mexican restaurant. I was a terrible waiter. Nonetheless, if I wanted to go to college, I had to find a way to pay for it. In my third year of college, my girlfriend became pregnant, and we got married. I continued to take classes during the day, and 6 or 7 nights a week I waited tables to try and make ends meet. I knew this wasn't sustainable. One day, I went down to the career counseling center at the University of Houston to explore career opportunities that would provide for my family. On the bulletin board, there were 2 lists: one with the most job opportunities for college graduates and one that ranked the salaries for those degrees. Accounting was at the top of both lists, so I switched my major to accounting.

My Badge of Honor in Accounting

In my first intermediate accounting class, the dean of the business school impressed upon us how important the role of an accountant was. We were told that only the top students would succeed in accounting. He explained how our financial markets depend upon transparent and reliable financial information, and how businesses rely on accounting information to make important decisions necessary to innovate, grow, and prosper. I was sold.

Over the next couple of years of coursework, I enjoyed learning the language of business—accounting. I found the logic behind financial accounting procedures fascinating and the importance of the information meaningful, in a story-telling kind of way. Accounting has always been more than a career for me. I've found meaning and purpose in the nobility associated with the profession; accounting is one of the only jobs requiring that you hold the public interest over that of your clients, meaning that your role in the business world is a key component to building a brighter future for the public and your clientele.

Better to Have Loved and Lost...

After graduation, I went to work at Ernst & Young (EY) in the firm's audit and assurance practice and with the Emerging Growth Market (EGM) practice. I loved working at EY. In the EGM group, I worked with smaller companies and gained diverse experience, technical expertise, and consulting exposure. The professionals I worked closely with were incredibly talented, dedicated, and dynamic. Notably, the partners weren't afraid to roll up their sleeves. During my fourth year at the firm, in an effort to find a better balance between work and personal life, I took a job with a smaller firm in Houston as an audit manager. After a couple of years at the firm and another couple of years in the internal audit department for a large oil company, I realized how much I missed working at EY. I found my way back to EY and picked up where I left off with the EGM team. What attracted me back was the dynamism and excitement of working on emerging growth companies.

In 2002, the Sarbanes-Oxley Act ushered in significant changes to the profession, and it impacted all public accounting firms. Notable changes included stiffened independence requirements and the requirement to audit the internal controls of public companies. In an effort to marshal resources to take on the added internal control audit work for the firm's largest clients, the EGM group began to wither away.

The prospect of auditing large public companies' internal controls was not something I was particularly interested in. The position I loved so much vanished before my eyes.

Smokey the Bear, a Bit Too Late

It was at that time that Halliburton recruited me to leave EY and become their director of technical accounting. In that role, I reported to the company's chief accounting officer (CAO) and was responsible for identifying, researching, and resolving technical accounting and auditing issues. During my interview with the CAO, we discussed, at length, the impact and importance of Sarbanes-Oxley, the changing role of the auditors, and the future of the accounting industry. The profession was under a microscope, and it was incumbent on public companies to have the necessary technical accounting expertise in-house. The profession wasn't the only thing under a microscope. Halliburton was too. My interviewer explained that as the director of technical accounting, I was supposed to be like Smokey the Bear. As Smokey the Bear, my job involved putting out fires and preventing them by training the company's accountants and elevating the accounting department's technical competencies. This was all part of what he called "building a world-class finance organization." It was my job, he said, to keep his name out of *The Wall Street Journal*.

The problem was, in February 2005, that I was walking into a place that was already up in flames! For years leading up to my hire, the company struggled to avoid bankruptcy and neglected to make necessary investments into their accounting and reporting department. With other priorities, senior management didn't make necessary investments in their accounting systems and people. They had essentially been winging it.

Unfortunately, they had been improperly recognizing revenue for many years after failing to adopt the Securities and Exchange Commission rules on revenue recognition in 1999. Put plainly, they were violating one of the most basic tenets of accounting: you can't recognize revenue until you actually deliver the product and provide services. Recognizing revenue on products parked in the company's warehouse was widely recognized as wrong and venal. When I brought the improper accounting to the attention of the CAO, he warned me that the politics of Halliburton would run me over and that I needed to be incredibly circumspect with the use of email. After explaining the dangers of email, he assured me the company would correct the accounting, that we would get the company back within the lines of what was appropriate. Unfortunately, that never happened.

Upon realizing that the improper accounting was material and would require the company to restate its previously reported financial information, they decided to ignore the problem. After that, the external auditor explained to me that they negotiated the issue away and told me to "save it for the subpoena." I knew I had to do more. I felt that it was my moral and professional responsibility to bring the fraud to the attention of the SEC. As the dean at my college had said many years earlier, the most important work an accountant does is to serve the public interest.

The SEC opened an inquiry into Halliburton's accounting, and I went on to fight for my rights as a whistleblower under Sarbanes-Oxley. SOX created legal protections where none had previously existed for individuals who report improper accounting and auditing issues. These protections were deemed necessary because, during the massive accounting scandals that created the need for radical change, Congress realized that all too often individuals who were aware of fraud were either too afraid to come forward, or when they did come forward they were ignored and/or retaliated against. Recognizing the critical role insiders can play in protecting the public interest, the new whistleblower protections were supposed to help prevent future accounting frauds. It took me 10 years to ultimately prevail, and the power of doing what was right always superseded any feelings of regret. My wife supported me every step of the way, and in the end, I am proud that my case has had a profound impact on that body of law, providing stronger protections for other would-be whistleblowers.

All too often, individuals look the other way. Decent people rationalize fraud. What matters most is not whether an individual is right or wrong, but that they have the guts to stand up for what is right. Organizations need to embrace a culture that encourages people to come forward with concerns. We need to expect more from those individuals: regulators, external auditors, audit committees, and management. We need to eradicate the model that continues to rely on those individuals with the most to lose and the least resources to protect the public interest.

Managerial Courage Has Its (Worthwhile) Consequences

Doing the right thing has its consequences. I had trouble finding a new job after being outed as the whistleblower. In 2009, during the height of the great recession, I struggled to find a job. I seemed to find myself in a recurring pattern. The initial interview would go great, but each and every time I elaborated on what happened at Halliburton, I never heard back about the job. That was until I interviewed with a company whose future was every bit as uncertain as my own, General Motors (GM). In 2009, GM had just filed for bankruptcy; the automotive giant was negotiating with the government for rescue. The government threw GM a lifeline. With it came a fresh start. This time, my interview went differently. During my interview with GM's CAO, Nick Cypress, we discussed, at length, my experience at Halliburton. Instead of showing me the door, he valued my experiences and was moved by my courage and high integrity. He told me I was the type of person that they needed to navigate their newest crisis, that he needed someone he could trust to tell him when something was wrong. I stayed with GM for over 7 years and played a key role in the company's emergence from bankruptcy. I went on to serve as the company's controller of US sales, service, and marketing, responsible for over $100 billion in annual revenue. I left GM in 2016 after prevailing in the Fifth Circuit Court of Appeals, ending my decade-long battle with Halliburton. This victory garnered national media attention, including interviews with *The New York Times*, *ProPublica*, *Bloomberg*, and *NPR Marketplace*. With media attention came opportunities to share my experience at prominent universities and organizations across the country. I grew excited about the opportunities to share my experience at conferences and universities.

These experiences brought purpose into my life and made me realize it was time to move on from GM. From there, I went back to grad school in pursuit of a new career in academia, sharing my experience and helping lay the foundation for the next era of accountants to fight the good fight. In 2015, I was invited to be part of Loyola Marymount University's Distinguished Speaker Series, and I fell in love with the place. Upon completing grad school, I accepted a position at LMU, and today, I am thrilled to share my experience with the students each semester. I try to get a few messages out to my students—besides the accounting rules and standards they need to know. As a professor, I teach the laws, rules, and regulations that individuals and organizations must follow. Yet, laws, rules, and regulations don't make a difference, nor do they fail. At the end of the day, the laws, rules, and regulations all depend upon the people who are called upon to comply, regulate, or adjudicate them. That is, individuals make a difference, and individuals fail. As a professor, I strive to teach future business leaders how they can make a difference.

Audits, Compliance, and Risk Management

External Audit and Internal Audit

It often seems like everyone wants to join the Big 4 audit after they graduate. According to some, joining that group is basically the only option. I understand the glamour of working in the top accounting firms, but I remember feeling anxious hearing the horror stories of working super long hours in audit. I did not start my career working for the Big 4—I did not even apply until I was stuck in my first job out of school. I knew that I needed more experience before I tried that culture. Turns out, the years I spent in public accounting—even though some parts of it were grueling—were some of the best and most eye-opening experiences. They allowed me to travel and learn about different businesses as I built my career.

An audit is an independent examination or evaluation of a company or organization. Audits can be performed internally or externally; both functions are complementary in an organization, but each serves separate purposes and has different focuses.

External auditors are generally employed by public accounting firms who serve many different clients, focusing on the financial condition of clients' organizations, and ensuring that the numbers are presented properly on financial statements. Internal auditors, on the other hand, work independently within an organization, as the company's watchdogs. Internal auditors protect the organization's value by ensuring that the company is not in violation of the compliance rules of their industry. They help to establish and validate internal controls, among other activities, and are uniquely positioned within an organization to serve an independent function, potentially fulfilling an advisory role to the company's audit committee and their board.

External auditors are like physicians: they conduct thorough examinations once a year, issue relevant opinions, and provide an overall diagnosis of a company's financial health in all material respects, mostly focusing on the numbers. Internal auditors, on the other hand, are like coaches: they focus on the tangible factors like daily habits and work within the company to provide ongoing guidance, ensure discipline, and sustain good habits.

External and internal audit functions are complementary—if a company has robust processes and procedures in their business operations, and has adequate preventive control measures in place to mitigate operational risks, then their financial records are most likely to be kept accurate and sound.

An audited financial statement adds credibility to a company, and leaders want to have that stamp of approval from an auditor to ensure a greater level of confidence with any financial statement users. Having a renowned firm audit and sign off on a company independently is different from presenting one's own financial statements. This is particularly important when the company is seeking investors, funding from a bank, or donors for a nonprofit organization, as it leads to more confidence from both parties in the numbers they are reviewing.

Working in the auditing industry can lead to many different career opportunities and advancements down the road. There is plenty of important and useful information in financial statements. Being able to interpret the numbers behind financial statements is an incredibly powerful tool that can help accountants become better professionals.

How Did We Get Here?

The accounting profession was largely self-regulated for a long time. Industry leaders proved that self-regulation was not sustainable as they led their corporations into the ground through self-serving means. In the late 1990s and early 2000s, top accountants and executives at Arthur Andersen/Enron and WorldCom were involved in incredibly complex accounting scandals, causing the 2 largest bankruptcies in history. Corporate greed and fraudulent activities in the top ranks of these companies destroyed many people's jobs, savings, and retirement. Ultimately, the world of internal audit, compliance, and risk management was created. Internal auditors today work to prevent catastrophes like those from ever happening again.

Industry authorities have created and implemented many laws and rules over the years to enforce effective corporate governance and best practices within an organization, with the goal of protecting investors and public interest. Most public organizations today deploy 3 lines of defense: the businesses in the first line, risk management and compliance professionals as the second, and internal audit as the third, all of whom work very closely together. An organization is like a human body; your outer skin layer, your cells underneath, and your immune system each serve an important role to defend and protect you. The ideal environment for successful businesses includes clear roles and responsibilities, well-documented policies and procedures, and, of course, integration across systems to promote transparency.

Most internal auditors and compliance and risk management professionals have an accounting background because the skills and experiences associated with accounting are highly respected, valued, and relevant to the internal audit position. Oftentimes, accountants are trained to be incredibly analytical, and data- and numbers-oriented. They have a certain business acumen and critical thinking skills that allow them to detect anomalies and inquire further. Fundamentally, though, internal auditing is not a typical accounting-based function. It extends well beyond the technical accounting of finance mechanics and analytics and looks at the organization and business as a whole. Thus, to succeed in these roles, one must understand and interpret information and resources and communicate their findings to senior management and committees.

Recognizing the importance of internal audit, risk management, and compliance is easiest if you think about the role these accountants play in combating financial scandals and illegal financial actions within and across companies. The importance of these accountants cannot be overstated: a lack of internal controls is not only illegal, it's also incredibly dangerous for a company.

Working in an external or internal audit can be a very valuable learning experience. If you are interested in learning about how a business is run, and everything financial statements, working in audit presents an incredible opportunity to talk about the business and the industry as a whole.

It also provides accountants with information that can be used to determine how the company can do better financial reporting, disclosures, internal controls, and other actions to ensure they align with the most up-to-date best practices in the industry.

When you audit a company, your work extends to all members of the company, and each bit of information you accumulate helps create the professional that you become. The experience associated with auditing a company cannot be replicated in training and, more importantly, cannot easily be quantified. When you view your first audits as learning experiences—opportunities to develop and master technical and soft skills—the foundations you build will stay with you forever.

Auditors are required to carry out their work independently, with strong ethics and sound judgments. The nature of an audit exposes the auditors to the sensitive details of a company. It is important that they carry professional skepticism when inquiring about personnel or management, or looking at general information. They also need to remain strong in their understanding of right and wrong, good and bad practices. Aside from the technical accounting and auditing skills taught in school and instilled at company training, what makes a good auditor is strong business acumen—having common business sense or being business-savvy. In other words, they understand and connect a wide array of competencies and knowledge in their awareness of business. Both verbal and written communications are also very important; auditors are constantly talking to different levels of employees and departments.

It is important to be able to communicate effectively and concisely to highlight the important key points, and simply explain complex issues and ideas.

If you are interested in learning about business as a whole and seeing the big picture, an audit career can offer a great opportunity to get that experience—whether as an external auditor with clients, as an internal auditor working in-house, or even as a risk management or compliance professional for one organization.

Tomoko Nagashima and Marco Glisic are both audit partners featured under the external audit discipline, while Bob Hirth and Andrew Raftis represent the internal audit, risk management, and compliance discipline. The industry continues to evolve and change. As such, the most important trait of an audit professional is the ability to adapt to constant changes in the industry and in businesses to be able to best serve clients.

As you will see from reading insights and experiences from the featured experts, an audit career can be a stepping stone to your career, or it can be an evolving career on one track. Either way, that experience can serve your career in ways that you may not have imagined.

5

Connect and Celebrate the Global, Brilliant Minds

Tomoko Nagashima

AUDIT PARTNER AT
PRICEWATERHOUSECOOPERS

Tomoko is currently the audit engagement partner at one of the Big 4 accounting firms in Los Angeles. When I first moved to New York City in 2006 to join their alternative investment practice, Tomoko was one of the few Asian partners I had the pleasure to meet. All these years later, I still remember and appreciate her kindness. She regularly took time out of her busy schedule to give me the guidance and support I needed. It meant a lot to me, especially as a newcomer to the firm and to the city. Most people who have worked with her described her to me as tough and intelligent: she always listens intently, speaks last, and asks intelligent questions.

Over the years, in addition to fostering client relationships and mentoring relationships with her coworkers, Tomoko has been a champion of the diversity and inclusion effort. In fact, she has served on the board of Ascend in Los Angeles, one of the largest, nonprofit Pan-Asian organizations for business professionals in North America. After nearly 3 decades of global professional experiences in accounting, she has made strides not only in the accounting profession but in diversity and inclusion efforts as well. Great organizations are made unique through their diverse culture and the blend of talents they have recruited from different backgrounds, experiences, perspectives, and values. Many organizations see the benefits of promoting a diverse culture that is open to sharing knowledge and experience and have mentoring programs in place to support their employees' professional growth. I truly believe diversity leads to innovation, creativity, and a stronger workplace, and I am excited to see leaders like Tomoko continue to lead the change by example.

Globetrotting Middle Schooler

I was born in Tokyo, although, throughout my childhood, my dad's job took us all over the world. The intense travel and relocation meant that I learned to adapt (and blend in) from a young age. We moved to Houston when I was 8, where I was held back a year because I hadn't mastered English just yet. I was shy and desperately wanted to fit in. I felt isolated from many of the kids in my class—a feeling that lingered until my dad's job took us to our next destination.

My mother impressed upon me that my childhood was an opportunity to find my passions and release energy in a productive manner. Sleepovers were limited in favor of a variety of lessons and after-school activities. Through these planned activities, I was exposed to a wide array of interests and hobbies and learned to make the most of the time I had. I certainly wished that there were more sleepovers in there, but my childhood provided a level of support and extracurricular rigor that developed alongside my international mindset.

No one in my family was in the accounting field. My extended family members were all involved in the business world, though, mostly in leadership positions. Through them, I developed an interest in the impact of leaders on employees, business development, and growth. I stumbled into the field of accounting during my undergraduate studies. I graduated from college with a double concentration in finance and accounting. Looking out of college into a struggling economy led me to want a job with stability. Quickly, I earned my CPA license and began my journey in the accounting field, starting my career working at one of the prominent Big 6 accounting firms at the time (currently Big 4).

Auditing Is a Client-Focused Business

Auditing, at the end of the day, is a client-facing and client-serving business, presenting accountants with a unique challenge in the world of auditing. We have to balance the public interest with our clients' specific goals and expectations, while also maintaining an independent perspective. The daily interactions with different personalities, plus the challenge of doing the job well, is a unique blend I'm so grateful to have every day. The constant learning is what continues to drive me to stay motivated and excited about my profession and firm.

Listening is the key to succeeding in building relationships. Truly listening to the client is the first step toward building a great relationship. Taking responsibility for that healthy relationship, and being flexible and creative when problems arise, ensures a strong foundation of trust. From there, perseverance and transparency are key to maintaining the relationship over time.

Since my motivation is the protection of the public interest and the capital markets, my team sometimes faces tough issues to navigate with clients. Based on my experiences, these interactions can be quite challenging, particularly if there is disagreement with the client. When the strong foundation of a great relationship is grounded, though, the navigation of tough conversation comes more naturally. The process itself is still painful, and not easy, but can be more productive, and even potentially strengthen the relationship as a result.

Maintaining open communication is certainly important, but not at the expense of honesty. The client must understand that you have their best interests at heart. I always say, "You got to tell it like it is." Be transparent when there is an issue. The earlier we can raise it and address it in a collaborative way, the better it allows the relationship to grow. Relationships are a form of art, not a science. This skillset will be developed with time and experience; don't expect it to click automatically.

Professional Value of Diversity

Nearly 3 decades ago, I was one of very few Asian staff in an audit entry class of 120 in New York. Starting off, I was my own worst enemy. I thought that because I thought, spoke, or acted differently than others, I was wrong. I actively tried to convince myself to blend in more. The notion that I would have to act and be like the "majority" to succeed instilled fear in my young self. I needed to constantly remind myself that diversity of thought is integral to sustainability in client service and communal growth that strengthens the organization. One habit I used was writing lists. On one side of the page, I would list things that were keeping me from being who I am; the other side listed why I should continue to voice my different perspective. Writing things down in this way kept me organized and focused on the positive side.

Time after time, through different engagements I was involved in, I realized the professional advantage of having a unique background, along with my values of keeping an open mind, exercising patience and empathy, and truly getting to know, accept, and collaborate with someone totally different from me. It felt incredibly empowering when I was able to leverage my cultural background to create successful strategies. I am pleased that I have found my place within my company, and the accounting field, having done so with pride in where I come from.

My advice to anyone struggling with their identity and the stereotypes around it would be to avoid dwelling on the barrier others place in front of you. Your background equips you with a specific power and a unique point of view. There is a beauty in coming from a different culture and background. Your diverse personality means that you contribute to a diversity of thoughts and perspectives. Nourish the confident cheerleader in you, not your own worst enemy. It's okay to come to the table as you are. Optimism and keeping a positive perspective will get you far in mindset and action.

Another big thing for me is consulting those I trust when making big decisions, dealing with difficult situations, or feeling like I'm stuck in a rut. It's always great to have a circle of advisors that I use as my sounding board when I get into a rut to express what I'm going through. They're always there to provide a listening ear, some advice, or even critical feedback. My personal "board of directors" is composed of family members, friends, coworkers, and mentors. I highly recommend creating your own!

International Accountant

In the professional world, I have been fortunate to be able to live and work in a number of different cities: New York for 11 years, Tokyo for nearly 4, and now Los Angeles for over 12 years. The firm gave me an opportunity to work in Tokyo when I was a manager/senior manager; in this role, I gained a global experience that I added to my toolbox.

I find that some things are the same no matter where you are. Since I stayed with the same organization in all of these locations, we always spoke the same firm language and followed the same processes and audit methodology. As a global firm, we're able to consistently bring our values to the forefront regardless of where on the globe our work is being conducted. Serving clients, and putting them first, remains at the helm, no matter where!

There are, of course, some differences between these locations. From a business cultural perspective, Los Angeles and New York are contrasted. I have personally found that New Yorkers are more forthcoming, telling you like it is when there are issues, whereas in Los Angeles interactions and communication style may be more passive in general. It's exciting to be able to experience both of these realities and find my place within the global field.

Through these experiences, I've learned how to be adaptable and effective in my client relationships. Listening is certainly the foundational skill to surveying clients in a successful way, and taking care of the people on your team working alongside you should always be a priority. I'm grateful for having the opportunity to learn this around the world.

Having Someone Go Up to Bat for You

Mentoring and sponsoring play a critical role in almost everyone's professional career. It is important and comforting to have someone who has gone through the motions of the business world, understands the real challenges and struggles, and is able to provide the support and guidance that is needed. Sponsorship is somebody who really goes up to bat for you, mostly behind the scenes, to make sure that you are set to succeed or take on the next role. Mentorship is somebody who is there to provide advice but may not go the extra mile as a sponsor would.

I find happiness in serving as a mentor to a number of less-tenured professionals. As my mentor and sponsor had done for me, I look to pay it forward to create future leaders. In terms of sponsorships, I am more selective. I put my all in sponsoring any individual and their career, and therefore I take my time getting to know an individual further to assess their talent and capabilities. Being a sponsor is hard because you have to believe in the person and go to bat for them, pounding the table to make sure the person gets an opportunity, recognition, or position you think they deserve. The difficulty comes with a level of excitement, though, because it's also very rewarding. I am a sponsor only for those whom I truly believe deserve the end goals I am going out to bat for, so I feel passionate about being a sponsor. I'll hit a home run for them in every incident.

In our firm, you need an official sponsor to become a partner. Becoming a partner is competitive, and only for those who reached a certain senior level and have proven to be high-performing individuals with strong skills all around. One of the partners, when I was a manager, took me under his wing. He then sponsored me throughout the partner admissions process to become a partner; he guided, challenged, and supported me with different viewpoints, constantly providing me with endlessly valuable personal and professional advice. He was a great resource to me, and I truly valued that sponsorship and mentorship. I also recently found out about numerous co-sponsors who were working on my behalf behind the scenes. I found out only on the back end, after I made partner, that there was an army of partners going out to bat for me, without any recognition, just because they thought it was the right thing to do. It feels great to have that.

The surprise of my colleagues and supervisors going up to bat for me anonymously underscores a point about the workforce more generally. What people have to say about you matters. Every action that you take—every good (or bad!) deed that you do—will come back. I harness that power as a reminder to always be helpful to others, act as a team player, and do the right thing. People are always looking. Give them something good to say.

6

Build a Blissful Work around the Life You Want

Marko Glisic

AUDIT PARTNER AT GREENGROWTH CPAS

Marko is the audit partner at GreenGrowth CPAs, one of the top premier cannabis full-service CPA firms in California. Marko shared his journey from his upbringing in Serbia, to his move to America, and his transition from corporate life to become a business owner. After overcoming some internal barriers, he was able to take all his learning from different cultures and apply them to his work in client services.

Family is always his main focus. Instead of choosing between returning home and staying in the US, he utilized technology to create the lifestyle that he wanted, one that blended the best of both worlds. He built his practice with his brothers and can afford to travel home whenever he wants for however long he wants! As for his career, leaving a promising and comfortable career path to step into the uncertainty of entrepreneurship takes a lot of courage. Marko is proof that once you step out into the unknown, you may find that you are able to create innovative solutions for clients and find levels of success that weren't possible before. Life is what we make of it; it's never easy, but when you find your rhythm, it's not only rewarding but a very fun journey. And it just keeps getting better!

Step Out to the Whole New World

I was brought up in Serbia, alongside conservative family values, which pushed me to be disciplined, work hard, and do well in school. My father was my biggest influence growing up. He was a chemical engineer and worked in the upper echelons of one of the biggest export companies in Serbia. I respect and look up to him, and when I was younger, I wanted to be just like him. I dreamed of doing something big. I didn't know exactly what—accounting certainly was not the first thing on my list—but seeing my father excel inspired and drove me to pursue my career with excitement.

In Serbia, we watched movies about American culture and became fascinated with the United States as "the land of opportunities." In my junior year of high school, my father told me about an opportunity to participate in an exchange program with the United States. Although travel between the (formerly communist) Serbian state and the United States was uncommon in 2004, I decided to take the plunge. With a world of uncertainties ahead of me, I enrolled in the program and was placed in Arkansas.

Once I graduated from high school in Arkansas, I followed in my older brother's accounting footsteps by enrolling as an economics major, first in a community college in Chicago, and then at UCLA. I loved how principle-based and logical economics was, how it functioned as a body of knowledge that I could study and understand. I took financial accounting and saw the same principles: if you understand the economics of transactions, and build up a base in financial accounting, you can often figure out how to record properly. I graduated in 2010, entered a difficult job market, and eventually found my way to an audit position with Deloitte.

At Deloitte, I worked in a lot of middle-sized companies without an industry focus. There were not many billion-dollar publicly traded companies back in the day. It was neat to work with many different types of clients. I did a lot of work in consumer business and for Dole, the billion-dollar fruit and vegetable food company. I did tech too. As I saw Silicon Beach coming about, I worked with startups in California. These jobs were awesome because they helped make my later transition to the startup cannabis industry in California seamless.

My goal when I first started at Deloitte was to move up and get to the top, just like my father who had one company his entire career and slowly worked his way up to his current position as CEO. I made it to the senior management level, but I quickly got bored. I decided to chart my next steps forward.

Lifestyle of Choice

From junior year through my rise at Deloitte, I became grounded to life in America, and visited Serbia only in a limited capacity, no more than 2 times a year. Although I enjoyed my own life in America, I really wanted a lifestyle that would allow me to visit Serbia for extended periods of time. I missed my family, and I missed my home. In 2015, when my mother passed away from cancer in Serbia, I was forced to seriously consider returning home. How could I balance family and work? I struggled with the idea of leaving the United States for close to 2 years before making a final decision.

During those 2 years, I explored the idea of starting my own business. I watched YouTube videos and found free resources online to start my own company. I decided that this was going to be something I would do, and excel in. My evolution from employee to entrepreneur had begun.

Let's Take This Higher

I eventually started a tax compliance company, exclusively for the cannabis industry, with my current business partner, Derek. I admire Derek as one of the truest entrepreneurs; he also stepped off the Big 4 and was one of the early movers in the growing cannabis industry. Because we focused exclusively on cannabis, our company was one of very few in the space offering tax compliance work for business returns. Leaping into developing our own business freed us from the constraints of being physically tied to one location.

Entering the cannabis space as early as we did set my team and me on a path to success. Initially, we worked strictly on tax compliance. Our business model, with its niche, focused on the rapidly growing California cannabis industry and connected nicely with the work I had done at Deloitte. In cannabis, there are cultivators (which is similar to agriculture), there is processing work (which is close to the work I had done in food manufacturing), and then there are the entire dispensaries (which are similar to my work in retail). For me, industry-wise, it was a very relatable and easy transition.

Over the years, we began to add on outsourced finance and accounting services to ensure clients were in compliance. In my position as audit partner, I've seen so many of the same type of business that I have a truly concrete understanding of how they run.

Looking at a client's business as an outsourced CFO allows me to engage with a higher level of consulting, and ask: Do you have the right level of employees? Is your cost structure out of whack? Why is your monthly payroll 1.5 times more than the average of other cannabis companies? What is your average transaction amount? How does it compare to the competition? I could almost immediately know what could be improved upon just by glancing at their key performance indicators. Over time, it became easier for us to advise clients and explain exactly what their financial potential could be transformed into.

The best (and in my opinion, only) way you can get to this high-level analytical point is by working in a niche and looking at thousands of the same type of financial documents. Spending the time to become an expert allows you to deliver the unique, highly qualified consulting that makes any entrepreneur successful. We're now getting to the point where we've stopped adding new services and are focusing on providing premium and value-added services to our clients, such as fundraising and financing, to increase our pricing. Our experience within the industry adds tremendous value to our clients.

Importantly, the regulation of the cannabis industry requires an immense amount of attention to rules. We're certainly not compliance experts in the entire cannabis field, but we know the financial aspects pretty well. Cannabis companies are targeted heavily by lawyers. Every year, there's at least one big tax court case involving the regulations and risks of cannabis. It keeps the industry interesting.

To me, the biggest challenge, and the most enjoyable part of running your own company, is hiring and training people while designing systems and processes for them to use. Right now, for example, we're documenting every single process we work on. From the sales cycle, to marketing work, to service deliveries, to client deliverables—everything gets documented. The documentation created a system for our company to hire and train people to understand and follow the clear and effective processes we've created.

These days, especially in entrepreneurship, where you are doesn't really matter in terms of how you can conduct business. I found that you can organize your life to have flexibility through global business. I ended up building this reality for myself through our company.

Once we were up and running in the United States, I expanded my business by combining my work in California with my 2 older brothers back home in Serbia. They're super smart accountants and I trust them in handling the Serbia business efficiently. From phone calls to Zooms, we stay connected on a daily basis. The resulting ease of balancing family and work life has been both comforting and fulfilling.

I find that when looking at your life goals, focus on the lifestyle that you want to live. Where do you want to be? Who do you want to be around? How do you want to work? If you define these expectations for yourself, you can build your business around these ideas on your own terms. Otherwise, you may be building your life around your job, leading to a neglect of things that matter, like quality time spent with loved ones. Creating a life that works around your priorities should always be a top goal; identifying these priorities is the first step.

Anyone reading this should know that starting your own company is as easy as deciding to do so. If I can do it, so can you. Start looking up the first steps on YouTube. Read blogs. Reach out to entrepreneurs you admire on LinkedIn. It's a fantastic community, and you can really find yourself here coming from accounting, or really, coming from anywhere!

A Change of Perspective

When I came to the US for the first time, it felt like a honeymoon. I was traveling, experiencing southern perspectives, and seeing new things every day. The reality, however, did hit after a couple of months, and with it came doubts about if I wanted to stay. My exchange program in Arkansas was nothing like what I expected America to be. I had seen the glamour of the big city lights in the movies, not the warm hospitality of a southern home. It was a gigantic cultural shock! My host family, an incredibly hospitable, kind, and generous bunch of southerners, helped me adapt, and I will always be grateful for that.

People in Serbia tend to have a more pessimistic outlook on life. I appreciate the hardships that many Serbians have experienced that led them to this mindset—famine, economic devastation, and more. However, I prefer to respect their perspective without adapting to it as my own. In fact, through my time in the United States, I learned to do the opposite. I found that being more optimistic had the potential to make things so much better for me. It took a while to adjust, but that experience was helpful as I, later on, became an auditor. My adaptation skills proved valuable as I continued to navigate across cities in the United States. I lived in Chicago, LA, and many other cities. Each place offered its own energy and uniqueness. With every move, I would re-learn and understand what was and wasn't socially acceptable.

When traveling, I would encourage all young professionals to seek a comprehensive understanding of the cultural mindset they are entering and engaging with. You can learn a lot from those around you, those you work with, or those who live nearby. Ask them questions about their worldviews, how they got there, and what they value. These questions may illuminate your personal worldview, values, and mindset in meaningful ways.

Beyond the Stereotype

Most people have the perception of accountants being introverted. Everyone has both introverted and extroverted characteristics, and different jobs and actions bring out various parts of these personality traits. I'd say I have evolved over time, holding onto and letting go of various traits that helped me succeed throughout my career. When I first joined Deloitte, for example, I was relatively shy. The environment was more conducive to introverted activities, which served me well. I am very analytical; being introverted really helped when I had to focus and think, especially when I was looking into the specific details of various audits. I realized quickly, however, that my career could benefit from increasing my extroverted characteristics—interacting and socializing with clients or peers not just to get information, but to stay connected throughout different networks and industries. You learn a lot by talking to different people. Sometimes, it even brings prospects in business.

I'd encourage all aspiring accountants to think about how the world is a lot bigger and more complex than what they are initially led to believe. There is so much more to the world of accounting. You can have your own business, work in a small or mid-size firm, or really permeate any industry. Moreover, accounting is probably the strongest, most foundational basis of information that you can learn. A lot of people start off in accounting and then turn to something else like fundraising, wealth management, consulting, mergers, acquisitions, valuation work, and more. Once someone has these foundations, they can branch out into so many different ways. You have to be willing to take a leap, enjoy the process, and start the journey. When you're ready to take the leap, find comfort in the fact that you can always go back. But be warned, almost nobody does! It's important to enjoy what you do, no matter what you choose. Everyone has their own path and way forward.

7

The Yellow Brick Road of an Ever-Changing Audit Career

Bob Hirth

SENIOR MANAGING DIRECTOR AT PROTIVITI, CO-VICE
CHAIR AT SUSTAINABILITY ACCOUNTING STANDARDS
BOARD (SASB), CHAIRMAN EMERITUS AT COSO, AND
FORMER PARTNER AT ARTHUR ANDERSEN & CO.

Bob is a great presenter and marketer. I first came across his work through a presentation on sustainability in the accounting industry, which I found incredibly meaningful. Bob spent over 2 decades working for Arthur Andersen (AA), one of the Big 8 accounting firms from back in the day. He truly made the most out of an audit career: starting as a junior person, traveling globally for assignments, and making it to the top as a global equity audit partner and advisory services partner.

Making partner is oftentimes seen as reaching the peak in auditing; Bob held the partner position in 2002 when his firm went through turmoil due to the Enron debacle. Unfortunately, the firm eventually ceased operations and relinquished its accounting firm licenses. While some individuals stop learning and growing when they reach the top, Bob embraced all the changes and obstacles and continued to step out of the comfort zone and challenge himself.

During those stressful and turbulent times, Bob moved along to join Robert Half International (RHI), and stepped into a new arena, building a new practice and brand in global business and risk consulting. He, along with a number of former AA partners, became the founding members of the new consulting brand Protiviti. At Protiviti, while continuously building a very successful consulting practice, Bob utilized the experiences he had accumulated from his decades of work and took many leading roles outside of the office in various accounting organizations, such as the Institute of Internal Auditors (IIA), state CPA societies, COSO, and SASB. He served 2 terms on the Standing Advisory Group (SAG) of the Public Company Accounting Oversight Board (PCAOB) and served as the chair for the IIA International Professional Practices Framework Task Force, which created the Core Principles of Effective Internal Auditing. His contributions and involvement in setting and improving accounting standards within the accounting profession are legendary and have had a great impact, extending not just to the accounting industry, but to financial markets as a whole.

Family

I come from a proud Swedish and German family. Swedes are practical, frugal, open-minded, and honest. Germans are disciplined and orderly. My parents taught me how to have fun in every situation, but not too much fun. They showed me the value of hard work. My childhood, and their work ethic, also imprinted an important lesson upon me: don't complain about something you dislike. Instead, do something about it.

My younger sister, fraternal twin brother, and I were granted plenty of freedom as kids, but we were also given clear boundaries. Being trusted to do the right thing and use good judgment taught me how to rely on my inner compass to make decisions. Knowing that hard work and success were expected of me pushed me to do well from an early age. My parents made it clear that each of us kids was expected to attend college. Both of them had gone to college in the 1940s, my father serving in the Navy in World War II, and were working professionals.

Childhood is a time to have fun and discover what you like and don't like, but it's also important to do well in school. Right or wrong, good or bad, grades are the accounting system for kids. It's the first time you understand that the world is keeping track of your performance, and it's up to you to maintain a high level in order to succeed.

I started working part-time at 16 and continued working throughout college, in addition to being an active member of the marching band, holding leadership roles in my fraternity, and being a sophomore advisor on a freshman dorm floor. I was an accounting major and got many credits studying German, but I prioritized social experiences as much as academics. Double majors were not popular or even always allowed, so I chose to get my degree in accounting.

Between my second and third years of undergrad, I wanted to make the most out of my accounting and German studies, so I arranged an accounting internship in Stuttgart, Germany, at an auto parts factory. I recognized that it would be the best time in my life to think and plan for different futures. I enjoyed the experience and realized that I could have a bright future in accounting. In my last semester in college, I interned full-time at Coopers & Lybrand. Once I graduated in 1976, I started my career at another Big 8 accounting firm at the time, Arthur Andersen (AA) in Dallas.

The Move Down Under

In 1988, AA asked me to move to Australia, and as part of that transfer, I would be promoted from senior manager to a global equity partner—a big promotion in responsibility and in compensation as well as becoming an owner in the firm. The opportunity was one of the biggest events in my business life, but it was a difficult decision to make, both personally and professionally. Sure, I was excited to be promoted into the global AA partnership, but I was also very scared. I had a world of questions to consider: Why me? Could I sell my house on time? Where would I live in Australia? How long would I be there? Is this a forever thing? What exactly would I do there in terms of work? Whom would my new clients be? What about my new boss? Would I be accepted in the office by colleagues? Would I make new friends? Would I succeed or fail? My thoughts were racing with both concern and enthusiasm. Ultimately, I made the decision to accept the new position and the new adventure.

My fears of failure proved to be unsubstantiated. It was a great experience. I grew tremendously, perhaps even more personally than professionally. I saw the sights, visited other cities and countries, met tons of new people, made new friends, and had my eyes opened to things I had never even thought about before. The experience made me a better professional and added a unique experience to my business resume.

The key lesson I learned during that time was to commit to success. That is, once the cards are dealt, make the most of it and have a plan to win. Understand what success will be in your own eyes and in the eyes of those who will judge and evaluate you. Make a solid plan to meet the goals and objectives set out for you and revise that plan if circumstances change. And they will always change. Most importantly, if the opportunity to move Down Under (or anywhere else for that matter) presents itself, take it with a smile!

My experiences in Australia echoed those in Dallas while also introducing me to novel experiences that expanded my horizons. The United States of America does not have all the best ideas. There are smart and capable people everywhere. While abroad, I cemented my understanding of the value of active listening, asking for help, and gaining feedback. Immersed in different cultural realities, I discovered that I could leverage my uniqueness as a foreigner. I recognized the value of being open to new ideas, developing relationships with as many people as possible, and adopting the culture of others when abroad. Bringing up questions, asking for help, and requesting feedback ensured that I would succeed in a novel framework of business. Moreover, I learned to turn to colleagues at all levels and understood that others may know more than me, even if they had less experience.

Importantly, some people and cultures simply have different priorities. I made it a personal task to figure out what my clients and the Australian offices cared about, what mattered for individuals and teams, and how to place myself in a role that would add value. By continuing to work within and around my Australian colleagues, I grew in tremendous ways. My 3-year experience overseas expanded my horizons and enabled me to return to the US to a wonderful location, office, and group of mentors in San Francisco, California.

Always Work Harder Than Everyone Else

Generally, my career goals were to continue to move upward and onward, taking on broader and more challenging roles to success. AA, during the fallout from Enron, ceased operations. Despite the firm ceasing operations and relinquishing its license to practice public accounting by its role in the Enron scandal, I still believe that it was one of the great firms I have worked at, and spent my career there because of the culture and people; in some ways, part of that legacy lives on through Protiviti.

I was one of the founding members of Protiviti and have now been with the firm for almost 2 decades. When Protiviti initially started, it was stressful, challenging, and exciting at the same time. I wore multiple hats, running the San Francisco office and the western region, while building and leading Protiviti's internal audit practice globally. I was also a member of the firm's operating committee, managing the firm's operations and setting its vision and strategy. In the midst of building the Protiviti brand, I found myself constantly searching for more ways to contribute and make a bigger impact outside of the office and in the accounting industry as a whole.

Over the years, I took all the opportunities to utilize my expertise through serving in many different key leadership capacities on various accounting organizations and boards, taking on broader challenges and also proposing and reinforcing necessary changes and improvements to different frameworks and standards.

In the first half of my career journey at AA, within one company, I worked my way up the ladder from being in a single US office to transferring to a non-US office, and later holding regional responsibilities. My transition and career at Protiviti have really allowed me to continue my career and progress in my professional activities. I founded and led a large part of a firm as a senior executive, and now hold a number of unique positions including co-vice chair of SASB and chair emeritus of COSO. Unless I go intergalactic, I feel like I've been able to participate and contribute to the broadest possible level in my chosen profession.

As I progress into my 60s (remember, 60 is the new 40), I'm proud to say that I have collaborated with hundreds of companies, met and worked with thousands of people, traveled for business to over 20 countries, worked in multiple industries, and made hundreds of large group presentations. This is no small feat, and it all comes back to my values and hard work. I love working with people to solve problems, I enjoy making presentations, and I find pleasure in recruiting. Once I have recruited employees and developed good people and hard workers, staying connected to them is also a source of excitement. Finding excitement in my work keeps me motivated to excel and pushes me through all of the hard work.

I always say that you should be the hardest worker in the room. Work as hard as you possibly can toward a goal that you value and be persistent—don't give up. It's a marathon and not a sprint. For me, success in the industry was motivation enough. Maybe your motivation is something different. Whatever it may be, the best way to get there is to keep guiding yourself through action and dedication.

Of course, you should make sure that the work you do is balanced against the fun that you have. I am always disciplined and thoughtful in how I prioritize and manage my busy schedule with my career and spending quality time with my family. I like being outside, and I like being on the move toward somewhere. One way that I like to relax is biking by the San Francisco Bay. I still manage to find time to ride more than 3,000 miles for most years; it's a great way for me to enjoy the scenery and also to think. I do my best thinking when I'm on the bike. Find, and constantly return to, those fun activities that make you happy.

Values

Honesty, integrity, respect, trust, and humility: these words spell out my last name, but they also represent my values—values that have made me successful. I always set aside time, no matter how busy I am, to reflect, set long-term goals, and make sure my actions are aligned to my values. By imagining the kind of person I want to be, I keep myself on track to *becoming* him. The best advice I ever received is to always work harder than everyone else and "make your own wake." This is what I've tried to do, and it has helped me greatly.

I advise students and young professionals to think about what they want their story to be so that they know what they are working toward. Accounting will help you succeed in almost every area, function, or field of interest—both business-wise and personally. Accounting is the way that all organizations "keep score," and the best, most competent, most successful clients I have worked with generally have had some accounting in their backgrounds. The most important characteristic, especially in the client servicing space, is knowing how to build relationships. It takes great listening skills—proactively listening to see what challenges or problems they are facing—and thinking about how you can help somebody. One of my favorite quotes is: "People don't care how much you know, until they know that you care."

8

Around the World in 3 Decades

Andrew Raftis

CHIEF RISK OFFICER AT UNISUPER, FORMER
CHIEF AUDITOR AT AXA EQUITABLE, AND CHIEF
COMPLIANCE OFFICER AT AIG ASIA PACIFIC

Andrew is currently the chief risk officer of a large Australian industry superannuation fund—the equivalent of a US 401(k) retirement or pension fund. Andrew's 3 decades of career journey can be summed up as a global adventure. His entire career has touched on almost all major regions across the globe. Born and raised in Australia, Andrew has lived and worked in Paris, Hong Kong, New York, Singapore, and Zurich.

Although traveling around the world with his wife and children was not always easy, Andrew stresses the importance of keeping an open mind when it comes to one's career. Andrew has been put into many new roles and positions and assigned with building various risk and compliance programs for global companies so that they could effectively keep up with the industry's changes. His work is inspiring: from building projects from the ground up to leading global teams and expanding global results for his companies and clients, Andrew has consistently demonstrated leadership and adaptability. While his technical skills, incredible dedication, and hard work certainly helped to ensure his success, his experiences of relocating, living abroad, and adapting to different people and cultures made him and his family much stronger. His broad global perspective, resilience, and adaptability shine through his character.

A Lesson in Persistence and Luck

For one summer break as a university student, I moved into a guesthouse in Seefeld, Austria, to try and get a job as a ski instructor. Well, 3 times I asked the head of the ski school, who was also the town mayor, about a job. I was rejected each time. I had done the work: I had taken ski instructor courses in Australia and California, skied around various Austrian and Swiss ski resorts taking lessons, and served my apprenticeship as a ski instructor at the Big Bear Mountain Resort in San Bernardino, California. I was about to give up. Most people would have told me to give up. The guesthouse owner where I was staying in Seefeld, though, was not like most people and told me to give it one more try.

So, I went to the mayor's office, again. By this time, the secretary knew me. She told me to go in and wait. It wasn't until the mayor walked in and sat down that he saw me on the other side of the room. He looked at me for a long while, shocked. Finally, in German, he said, "Okay. Come to the ski school on Sunday."

It wasn't a promise of a job, but it was a chance and a reward for my persistence. So, I showed up at the ski school meeting place. I was brushed to the side, some distance from the ski school management.

Suddenly, I heard an instructor calling out for an English-speaking instructor. The mayor just turned around and nodded. That was it. I was officially a ski instructor in Seefeld, Austria. My persistence and flexibility had paid off, and that was a lesson I took with me to many jobs after.

To be successful, you have to be a little bit lucky. But I've found that the more I practice, the luckier I get. The ski instructor job showed me that challenging myself and not giving up, combined with being in the right place at the right time, led me to great opportunities. No one gets anywhere by taking it easy.

Made in Australia

I was born in Melbourne to a middle-class family. My parents were professionals: my dad had a legal practice and my mom worked as a law clerk in the same office. I don't remember thinking a lot about what I wanted to be as a kid. I listened to a lot of David Bowie, kicked a football around, and hung out at our farm. I was most interested in history and politics. I did not particularly like school. I did not dislike it, but I just wasn't a *natural* as a student, and I found schoolwork rather boring. When I was 15, I took a year off school and traveled throughout Europe for 6 months with my parents. That experience truly shaped me and gave me a great global perspective.

Eventually, I enrolled at the University of Melbourne to study law and commerce. I enjoyed my time at university, relishing the sudden increase in freedom and the variety of people and perspectives on campus. I involved myself in team sports (even competing in InterVarsity), served as president of the ski club, and continued to work with different university activity committees. Although I was involved in a lot of extracurricular options, I focused mainly on graduating in law. Because of my parents, a law career was the only career option I understood.

I landed my first job out of university as a lawyer doing banking and securities, a highly competitive field in Australia at the time. I was proud and excited about finding a good job, but it became a bit too routine. After successful completion of the apprenticeship and passing professional exams in required subjects, I was admitted to practice in the Supreme Court. In Australia, that meant I could work as both a barrister and a solicitor. I started practicing banking law, seeing through the completion of properties, loans, and mortgages. I wanted to become a corporate lawyer and eventually move into management.

My very first task as a young lawyer was to write a business letter. We never went over how to write a business letter at university. In fact, I discovered that my work in the real world did not resemble what we learned at university at all. I realized, with shock, that I didn't know where to start. I looked at the files, and the secretaries helped me set it up, but I remember feeling so confused about how to write a simple business letter.

What style of language was I supposed to use? How should I address it and what were the formalities? With help, I was able to effectively create the first draft of a fairly simple letter of advice. My boss then helped me fine-tune it and explained the value of effective communication skills.

Presenting effectively to board members, senior management, or anyone is critical. Even if you're a wizard at accounting, not being able to clearly explain the risks and issues of concern can harm your likelihood of success. If there's one piece of advice I'd give to every young professional, it would be to focus on fine-tuning your writing and presenting skills early and often.

After only a few years of working, I joined a large Australian insurance company as a corporate lawyer. The company, National Mutual, was not big in American terms: the head operations were in Melbourne, with operations in 8 countries in Asia, and small operations in the UK and the US.

One day, my boss asked me to do some research on compliance. Always driven to do a thorough job, I created the best presentation possible. Pleased with my findings and the report I presented a few weeks later, he asked me to work on setting up the compliance program I had recommended. I protested. I had just taken up management of the commercial division of the legal department. He said he believed that I was best suited to make the program successful. Little did I know, then, that I was setting off on a path that would carry me for many years.

Entering Risk, Compliance, and Internal Controls

During the course of setting up the compliance program, I had to juggle many different issues. I was effectively starting with a clean slate. First, I had to come up with a way of prioritizing compliance issues. In 1995, Australia and New Zealand had jointly developed a risk management standard that was one of the first in the world. I used this risk management standard as the basis for risk rating all of the compliance and legal issues that the company had. I also referenced my audit coworker's model on control self-assessment and developed a large compliance self-assessment program so that all control obligations of management and staff could be assessed in the same manner. In this role, I learned about risk management, audit, and internal control assessment, all while applying the disciplines to compliance.

Who Knows What's Next?

I'm proud of starting a compliance program and later a control self-assessment and risk program from literally nothing and developing all of the assessment questions, risk guards, controls, and reporting to build an entire program aligned to compliance regulations and risk and control objectives. I realized that being open to change and growing continually leads to success. That's really how my career evolved—I kept learning and taking on more responsibilities in varied fields, outside of my direct educational experience.

My success is partly attributable to the fact that I didn't have an entrenched view of what I was going to be, and I have an interest in continual learning. I kept my options open, was flexible, and learned about the new areas and disciplines I became responsible for. Flexibility is likely to broaden possibilities in your career. My career has taken me and my family to many countries over the past decades. I was always very interested in different cultures and different countries, and I wanted to give that same experience to my children. Going international was not something that happened overnight. Rather, I had expressed my interest at the outset to the firm and my boss; I worked hard every step of the way and proved my abilities and leadership through key projects. I was selected when an opportunity finally arose after many years.

To anyone who is thinking about their career upon graduation, don't worry too much about getting a specific job. There's so much to learn at that point. Rather, find a reasonable job with a boss you respect and remain open to change. Only by working will you discover what you enjoy and don't enjoy, what you're good at and not. The first work experience will give you a solid foundation and discipline, but it's up to you to make it the best and continue to evolve.

I have been a chief compliance officer reporting to board audit and risk committees. As part of my role, I gained exposure to regulatory agencies, listing requirements, rating agencies and analyst reports, external auditors, and even external consulting firms. Because of this wide variety of experiences, I subsequently got roles as a chief risk officer, chief internal auditor, and financial controls director. Once again, the harder you work, the more exposures and experiences you get, and the more luck seems to favor you.

Internal Audits Go Global

Internal auditing is a well-established profession, as it has been around in a formal sense for at least 70 years. It contains a body of internationally accepted audit practices. As an internal auditor, one of the big advantages is that once you understand the internal discipline and the various requirements, you can apply your audit skills to any business in any country in the world, providing you with a great degree of career flexibility.

Of course, you always need to learn the particulars of the business in which you work, but your approach to doing internal audit work can generally be applied quite broadly.

If you are interested in being able to move to different cities, companies, or even countries, internal auditing offers a great opportunity to do so, particularly now in IT and cyberspace, where there is a huge demand for auditors, risk managers, and consultants with those skillsets. I was interested in working abroad professionally after my travels when young, and worked in the US and Austria as a student. I loved learning about foreign cultures, their history, and their different customs and beliefs.

I was very fortunate that my wife has an outgoing personality, enjoyed the traveling experience, and adapted extremely well everywhere we went. My work travels also meant that my children gained a global perspective and spent a significant amount of time in major cities worldwide. I wanted a great broadening experience for my children to learn about different cultures and values, as well as the way that businesses work, doing internships while at school and university. All the travels and experiences really helped my children develop their understanding of the world and their career goals.

As for me, I'm proud of the fact that I've been able to work in 5 different professional disciplines and brought together all of my expertise and viewpoint to build each on a global scale: legal, compliance, risk audit, financial control, project management, and all of the work in preparation for these jobs. I really enjoyed the international experiences and adaptation to working in different countries. I found, in the countries I worked, that the ways of working were usually vastly different. In Germany, meetings were punctual to the minute and dealt with business in an ordered manner, while in France meetings were always late, often chaotic, and not infrequently inconclusive. Yet, both countries have large successful international businesses and strong economies. In the US and Japan, the insurance industries are heavily compliance-driven and seem to be successful in spite of the burden of regulation. In Switzerland and Germany, high respect is paid to graduates from technical and trade colleges, as much as to university graduates. In some countries, high qualifications are almost essential for senior management positions, yet in others, experience has a higher value. Being adaptable, interested, and willing to learn is essential to success in foreign postings. One thing is certain: things will be done differently from what you are used to in your home country.

The World Of CFO Office And Financial Control

Financial controls are essentially how a company should effectively use its financial resources, e.g., cash, credit line, or liquid investments, to serve the company and its stakeholders. This is where the chief financial officer's (CFO) office comes in to establish mandates for direction, allocation, and monitoring for the several functions that follow.

How teams are structured depends on the size and complexity of the company. Individuals may wear many hats and serve different functions in one organization. Thinking about the actual work that financial and accounting departments engage in, we can pose a few key questions: What positions are there in the office that relate to the organization? How do these roles support and serve other departments? In what ways do they influence the daily business of the corporation?

Let's look at a more established company as an example: there are generally several teams under the CFO leadership, working on 3 key functions: controllership, financial planning and analysis, and treasury. Each team focuses on one function, meaning they engage with different mandates and expectations. Many accountants, myself included, have rotated between different roles and leadership titles within the CFO team. In fact, many big companies encourage this form of career adaptation to retain talents within the firm. Collaboration between these groups is one of the most important keys to successfully and seamlessly implementing and executing the strategic direction of the CFO.

I get asked this question a lot: what does a CFO do, and what makes a good CFO? There's a lot to unpack in that question. CFOs wear many hats, and they have the toughest job but also the most interesting (and fun)! They combine all of their skills and experiences and apply them strategically to the complex problems of their business in order to grow their company.

CFOs often have to manage many relationships internally with teams and externally with partners such as banks, vendors, regulators, and such. Moreover, they must manage the expectations of investors, stakeholders, and executives. It is important to have strong leadership, confidence, and assertiveness to succeed as a CFO. At the end of the day, everyone relies on the CFO—not only to present financial results, but also to guide the strategic vision of the company and make decisions. The CFO is expected to be able to communicate effectively with confidence and assertiveness to tell a complete story of the company through financial measures. They clearly identify the strengths, weaknesses, risks, and opportunities of the business to make sure they have the right strategic focus to take advantage of the good times and weather the bad times.

Generally, it takes years to build the competence and relevant experiences to be great. There's not one single path for CFO. Some come from backgrounds in accounting or audit, finance or law, engineering or math—the importance is having the right skills and character to be able to bring everything together, see the big picture in business and industry, and bring value and strategy to move the company forward.

I talked to Evelyn Foo and Shad Bien; they each have unique journeys and are in different stages in their careers. I hope they provide you with diverse perspectives on what it means to work in this field. Through different experiences and explorations, they each eventually found their path to finding meaning in their work, building teams, and helping their companies and businesses grow.

Although both Evelyn and Shad became something different than what they originally thought they would, they currently find purpose in their work and continue to make a positive impact. I cannot think of anything more satisfying and fulfilling than being able to achieve that in your career. You may have an idea of what path you are interested to pursue within accounting and finance, but I encourage you to keep an open mind and let your career unfold. You never know what opportunities may come your way, taking your career on an unexpected turn!

9

Risk, Resilience, and Determination to Hit the Open Road

Evelyn Foo

MANAGING CONSULTANT, FORMER PRESIDENT,
CHIEF FINANCIAL OFFICER, AND CHIEF
OPERATING OFFICER AT GALILEO

Evelyn is a seasoned financial services executive with over 3 decades of deep and broad experience in all aspects of the asset management industry. She started off with a seemingly traditional career path in one of the Big 6, PWC, and climbed up the corporate ladder in different areas in invest-ment banking until she was laid off for the very first time when she was in her 40s with a family. The layoff gave her the time and opportunity to do some searching, both personally and professionally. She was able to examine what she really wanted to do. She eventually stepped into a new and more visible executive role with a boutique firm, Galileo Global Equity Advisors, which, when compared to the global investment bank she was previously working for, was smaller in size. But the small team was mighty under her direction. After a decade at Galileo, she was able to lead the company to the next level.

She has served in the key roles of president, chief operating officer, chief financial officer, and board director. Evelyn accomplished everything from setting a strategic vision to guide the firm to growth and scale to product development, leading finance and operations strategies to identify gaps to improve and re-engineer processes and guide change management. This experience eventually led her to yet another new venture in her career in her 50s—to start her own consulting company. Her journey demonstrates the importance of risk and resilience, and the determination to step out of her comfort zone. She remained open to a whole new arena of opportunities professionally and personally and was able to discover that, when willing to explore what was in front of her, she was much more capable than she thought.

Moving across the Globe

My family and I emigrated from Taiwan to Canada in 1969 when I was 6 years old. My father left a prestigious role as the head of the Taiwan airport operations for Northwest Orient Airlines to seek a better life for our family. This sacrifice would spark my drive for success in this new country and a love for travel. My story isn't that much different than any immigrant to a new country, but accounting led me on a journey that has left an indelible mark on my life.

I was introduced to accounting when I was in high school. I considered it fascinating that financial information could be organized in a system to report on the financial well-being of organizations and individuals. I decided then that this would be my vocation going forward. My parents weren't pleased; they wanted me to become an engineer, a doctor, or a lawyer. I was undaunted. There was glamour and mystique to dressing up to go to a lofty office building, and I wanted to be part of it.

It's about How Many Times You Get Up, Not Fall Down

I failed my first-year economics course. It was a core course, and I needed it to get into the business program. I had coasted through high school without applying myself, and the stresses and expectations of the accounting major were brand new. Although the failure brought about a brief period of self-doubt, I quickly grew more determined to retake the class and get into the program. I knew that I could do it if I applied myself. I re-enrolled, passed the class, and completed my degree in 5 years. That early lesson in perseverance and grit set me up for success throughout my career.

All successful businesspeople have failed. In some ways, spectacularly. These failures, ironically, taught them the lessons necessary to reach new levels of achievement they wouldn't attain if everything came easy. They learned how to pick themselves up. They knew that if they were to stay down, they would miss the chance to grow and learn irreplaceable lessons that only failure can teach.

Take a Step Back

In my junior year of college, I took a gap year and worked at the junior level in financial firms, equipped with a desire to join the field of accounting and a passion for learning how an organization functioned. I learned to present a profile confidently and gained a deep understanding of the business environment. More importantly, my work reinforced my focus on pursuing accounting as a career after graduation. I was motivated by the concept of accounting as the lifeblood of an organization: the numbers are accumulated throughout the areas to determine all aspects of profitability. Accounting is a necessary function for every organization globally, which made the profession even more attractive, given my love of traveling.

Working within professional accounting during college allowed me to stand out in my applications as a postgrad, despite my B- GPA. I was accepted everywhere I applied and joined a public audit firm, which allowed me to participate in various industries, engage with senior executives, and explore different facets of key financial determinants. Had I not paused my education for the work experience, I'm not sure if I would be where I am today.

My experience working during college taught me that there are some lessons that can only be learned from experience. Stay curious and equip yourself with a positive attitude when approaching new experiences, and you might enjoy the journey along the way. Some experiences will be unanticipated. I say, bring it. You will learn from it and it will be valuable. Exposing yourself to new experiences moves you forward. You always want to be moving forward; you only look back to learn something. Once you've done that, you continue moving forward. Experiences don't bring you backward—they equip you with the lessons of lived history.

Put Your Hand Up. Often.

As a junior accountant, I remember feeling boxed in by the job role I was fulfilling. I craved more, so I asked for it. I raised my hand in my boss's office and asked for more opportunities and projects outside of my defined role. Little did I know that would be the first step to gaining access to gems of experiences. Choose the harder way. You'll learn more on that path.

Having the initiative to volunteer for new projects or tasks enriches your knowledge and exposes you to new and different aspects of a business or strategy. I say raise your hand. Often, and high. You have the capacity to create the career you crave within the job that you are fulfilling by acting outside of what is directly expected of you. Your job description is just a starting point. Having gone to university, you are smart. What's the worst that could happen if you take a risk and raise your hand? Keep this question in your mind to ensure that you keep moving forward. Worse comes to worst, you step away from the project you volunteered for and go back to fulfilling the role they explicitly hired you for. Sounds like a win-win to me.

Have confidence in your ability to take the risk and do so with excitement. Remember, you have very little to lose and everything to gain as you move forward in your career. Progress isn't always a straight path. You can take left and right turns along the way—just do so in a way that ensures you continue to learn and grow from the experiences you are having.

Unanticipated Twists Lead to New Opportunities

After the subprime crisis, I was transitioned out of a large company that I had spent 11 years in throughout my late 40s. Suddenly, I needed to dig back into my reservoir of confidence, positive thinking, and perseverance. I viewed the transition as a hidden opportunity to pursue another industry or role: what other choice did I have? Leveraging my network, I reached out to previous bosses and clients. One of my clients knew of a firm looking for a CFO. As CFO, I instantly became a key member of this small group and had the opportunity to perform basically every role in the company, short of picking securities in the portfolio. In this position, I learned US tax, GAAP, and SEC reporting. It was an education that was worth a million dollars that I didn't have to pay a penny for!

My accounting background opened up the ability to analyze the business from all aspects and gave me a unique perspective and insight to solve business challenges. I was able to make business decisions that the company relied upon with very limited resources. After 11 years of working at this company, sales of our product disappeared, and clients withdrew their monies from the existing funds. I talked to the owner about the specter of "winding down" and "cutting our losses." He disagreed and the 2 of us decided to part ways. I already had my next adventure in mind.

Freedom from Traditional Constraints

Although I've always been interested in the accounting industry, I don't consider myself a typical accountant. I've always been curious about how things work, from start to finish. My curiosity helped me excel in the smaller organizations I cultivated successful business models for. It also set me up with an entrepreneurial spirit that led me to start my own firm.

I never considered going out on my own until I did it. Funny enough, I obtained my first consulting client when I offered to help analyze profitability metrics free of charge! I thought taking the plunge would likely mean a reduction in salary, but I found excitement in the thought of earning my personal freedom and putting my experience into practice via consulting. I was told that before I could set up my own firm, I needed to have a sense in my mind of my value proposition to a client. What differentiated me from a crowd that would lead them to want to take me on? I made sure to solidify my value proposition before leaving my position at the firm and found 2 clients that dedicated themselves to my services. I knew the back-office pieces of accounting so well. I had gone through conversions, kept in touch with vendors, and sustained many relationships within the field that ultimately supported my leap into the consulting realm. I launched my consulting firm by curating profiled experience in operations, compliance, and finance to assist in complex transactions into a marketable and palatable service that my clients couldn't get anywhere else. I had experience in all the roles at the management firm level and watched investment products; I was able to offer organizations a commitment that came with my experience and views associated with those past roles.

Having my own firm means that I am paid to tell clients my advice, honestly and plainly. I don't have to pander to other people or office politics. I have gained personal freedom that leads my clients to appreciate me for me. Moreover, I enjoy having my own consulting company because I like bringing in and sustaining high-level excitement and energy. My creativity and personality were pushed to the side in the corporate world; starting my own consulting firm brought my creative and analytical sides together, allowing me to reconnect with my sense of self and purpose. Most importantly, I'm happiest when I'm really busy, and I'm having the best time right now.

10

Overcoming the Underdog Mentality

Shad Bien

STRATEGIC FINANCE AT UIPATH, FORMER GLOBAL
CONTROLLER AT ANDELA, AND US ARMY VETERAN

Shad is a tech-forward innovator with a strong background in running global financial operations, leading finance and accounting functions, and serving as a controller and strategic finance leader. He was able to combine his experience working on the West and East Coasts, running domestic and international financial operations, to successfully scale and transform teams that played key roles in various milestones of a company such as IPO, finance integration, and strategic investment.

Shad followed his father's footsteps and served in the US Army when he was 18. Despite a foundation of discipline and pride, he still had to overcome the feeling of being an underdog amongst the best and the brightest in the accounting field. As he progressed in his career, he continued to build not only skills, but character—both served him well as he rose up the ranks to lead bigger teams. It takes a lot of grit and perseverance to serve as a leader, managing global teams with many different cultures and personalities. Shad shares with us how he did it all.

The Commitment to Serve

I was born in Hawaii, the third of 3 siblings. My dad was in the Navy, and both my parents worked, so I quickly learned to do what I could on my own. I did chores, taught myself how to cook, and tried to take care of myself. My father was an immigrant from the Philippines who worked hard in the military but was dedicated to his family and unrelenting in his belief in the importance of college. When I was growing up, I would get so annoyed that it seemed like the only topic of conversation between us was college and what I was doing to make sure that I would get myself there.

I no longer view it that way. Now, I realize that with each of these conversations, he was planting a seed in me. He instilled in me a passion for education through this ceaseless dialogue, and it took root. Admittedly, I wasn't the best student when I was young, but math always seemed to make sense to me. In fact, I started getting teased about my math skills and tried to hide them.

I wanted to be independent, not a burden on my family. So, like many other determined young Americans, I joined the military when I was 18. I wanted to see the world, and most importantly, I didn't want my parents to have to pay for my education.

The military requires working weeks at a time without a day off—commitment is one of its founding principles. For me, this grew into a core of responsibility, discipline, integrity, and accountability. I went through the intensity of boot camp, a year studying to become a specialist, and then 2 years in Europe. Nothing about my early life led me to embrace taking it easy.

Falling into Accounting, Balancing Passion and Practicality

I began college in 2003, with a major in software engineering. At this early point of the creation of computer science courses, the work was extremely confusing, and I quickly wanted to explore other options. I liked the accounting classes and realized that there was a vast array of opportunities in accounting—be it public, private, nonprofit, or any industry. All companies and organizations need accountants. I recognized the value of this and saw it as a good foundation and a good career. I kept taking courses within the major. In this way, I kind of "fell" into accounting.

I recognized the importance of choosing a degree that could provide me with job stability. I wanted to be challenged to learn and grow; I also needed to be paid well. I believe that choosing your career requires balancing passion and practicality. I found that accounting was a logical career choice; the math made sense to me, and the job stability seemed to be remarkable—everyone needs an accountant! I felt good about it.

Overcoming Underdog Mentality

My experience on the West Coast taught me that employers didn't really care about what college you went to. They wanted to know, instead, about your involvement, experiences, and past positions, and the people you looked up to. But when I graduated from college and moved to a corporate position on the East Coast, it seemed like bosses cared more about what was written on paper. And all of my competition had very prestigious universities on their resumes. I felt like an underdog with my degree from the University of Hawaii.

Overcoming that mentality required dedication, focus, and hard work. I knew I wanted to be a controller, a CFO, and I was determined to get there. I knew that my experiences would shape me into being a unique candidate, separate from those Ivy League graduates. With patience and persistence, I climbed the ranks up to my dream role.

I overcame my mental obstacles and insecurities by focusing on growing toward my goals. Relaxing and collecting my pay isn't in my DNA; I actively pursued opportunities to be productively challenged. Work ethic is one of the most important aspects of anyone and it should be continuously refined and developed. It is a personal choice if you want to work hard or not; take it on as a task to develop your personal work ethic and stay hungry for more. If you do what makes you happy, this will likely come naturally.

In the past 7 years, I have been heavily involved in many different aspects and capabilities in controllership and strategic finance in building, transforming, and scaling several growing startup technology companies. I managed treasury and tax operations, led the global implementation of several key ERP solutions, established a strong global close process, and successfully completed many audits. I also led financial diligence and integration of strategic investment, as well as assisted with readiness workstreams to prepare for a potential IPO. I consider myself to be quite well-rounded and believe that being well-rounded is one of the keys to having a successful career. My abilities mean that the CFOs of my companies rely on me for practically everything: closing deals, raising capital, building off of systems and implementations, growing teams, engaging with external parties, meeting with attorneys, and the list goes on. It turns out that, contrary to the advice to "relax," the thing I enjoy most about a job is being challenged and continuing to learn. Often, I'm handed tasks that I have never tried before, and I take them on with pride and a sense of excitement toward the challenge.

In my role in controllership and strategic finance, I often refer to my team as financial operations. We are not just the accounting team; the word accounting draws up images of introverts in back offices. We are more than that: we think about all the different process cycles, cross-functional departments, and stakeholders. My financial operations team at Andela was the strongest team in the company; we had a seat at the table and our voice mattered. We worked through treasury functions, domestic and international financial operations, tax operations, financial reporting teams, and the back order to cash—one of the most important aspects of any business. I take pride in leading teams and being able to speak up about our accomplishments. We choose aggressive projects that cover more than just accounting. Large scale implementation and project management allow us to show the value of the work, particularly through our unique financial lens.

The Importance of Company Culture

Location and company policy play key roles in creating a company culture, which impacts how you feel on the job. On the West Coast, the people are normally more relaxed, and the companies tend to be more progressive, forward, and innovative—especially in the Bay Area. When I moved to New York in 2013, I stepped away from the venture startup space to go work with a software company. The company was based on tradition and legacy rather than innovation, and the culture reflected that. I instantly knew it wasn't a great fit for me, but I stuck it out, and the experiences taught me a lot about how to navigate office politics, how to act in tough situations that may require you to be combative, and most of all, perseverance.

It was also through that position, and interaction with company culture as an important point in my career, that I knew that I needed my voice to be valued; I recognized the importance of being thoughtful and particular about the companies that I want to join. For example, I value diversity, and I will always check the diversity present in the leadership of a company before applying or meeting with them. There should be a variety of ethnicities and genders present for me to consider it. My last company, Andela, had a huge presence in Africa. The majority of the 2,000 employees were African, and there was a culture of diversity and acceptance. The company welcomed honest discussions and fairness; it held pride events and women's leadership conferences, and the general atmosphere was one of favorable reception. This ambience really kept me there, feeling good about my work and the people I was working for.

It's important to recognize that no matter what lifestyle you lead or where you are in your career, you will face adversity and challenges. You have to be able to ride the ebbs and flows of life up and down; developing grit can help with this. I recommend the book *Grit: The Power of Passion and Perseverance* by Angela Duckworth, which focuses on how having that grit to really face challenges head-on, and be fearless, might take you even further than having book smarts.

Passing the Baton + Mentorship

As a leader, I find that giving young professionals the opportunity to present early is imperative. I have done many presentations in front of many different audiences in different companies, and I encourage my younger colleagues to take some time to really develop the executive level of experience in how to communicate and explain your work to leaders. It requires knowing your audience, your material, and all the supporting information. To encourage this, I ask younger members of my team to present a few slides at the global monthly meeting, where each country goes over its financials. This gives each member of my team experience in talking to the VP controller, CFO, and other important individuals. These opportunities allow them to gain value in leading and presenting. Before they start, I go over talking points and explain how natural it is to be intimidated when you enter a room filled with senior C-suite executives. Asking your team to present will encourage them to become more proactive. It's important to allow them the opportunity to speak up, lead meetings, and answer questions about your team. It helps to prepare them by going over talking points beforehand and providing positive affirmations.

I have also often been placed in the mentorship position. When companies or individuals pair people up, it often feels like an obligation or chore. I find that people naturally gravitate toward each other when they have similar experiences at work or through some sort of professional organization.

I appreciate being the mentee too; my mentor Ed Nakano is from Hawaii, has also served in the military, and has been a CFO of C.S. Wo & Sons for over 30 years. His daughter served as my manager when I worked at a public accounting firm, and I scheduled lunch with him. We had a great conversation, and it was easy to connect quickly because of our shared military background. This type of mentorship will provide the most value for both individuals.

Some Parting Advice

"Just relax and collect your pay" is the worst advice I've ever gotten. I can understand the appeal; who wouldn't want to land a decent job and coast? Yet from a young age, I learned that hard work is actually what gives life meaning. Do what makes you happy. You know yourself best. Develop grit, passion, and perseverance, and you will go a lot further in life than if your toolbox has only grades. If you're in college, though, get good grades. Try and maintain a 3.5 GPA. This will keep you competitive when the job market opens—especially if you are looking to join the Big 4 accounting firms. Employers are evaluating your college performance on this number, and with a high GPA, you may have competing offers, allowing you more freedom and options to choose how you wish.

To stand out from the average employee, work on your interpersonal skills. Building relationships cross-functionally with other people in different departments—even if it is just grabbing a coffee—will have great returns. There may come a time when you need help from them; if you have developed a relationship prior, they will likely be eager to assist.

With all of my advice about hard work, I want to be clear that I believe in balancing your life. You have access to email and work from practically anywhere, but that doesn't mean you should work on weekends and ignore your loved ones. Take the time to do the things you want to do. Try not to work weekends—spend time with your family and loved ones. Don't make sacrifices; make time for the things that matter. Be flexible with your schedule, know your priorities, and be smart about when to put work aside.

In today's world, it is the unfortunate reality that no matter how hard you try, it will be extremely difficult to keep up with all of the latest news—especially in startup companies. Accept the fact that you will not know everything all of the time; it makes putting your phone aside a bit easier. No one person is aware of all of the constant improvements and changes happening in the industry, so don't expect that of yourself, either.

The World Of
Taxation

As Benjamin Franklin famously said, 2 things in life are certain: death and taxes. Taxes are inevitable; owing taxes can lead to severe penalties, seized properties, or even jail time. That's why tax accountants are so important: they make sure that taxes are filed timely and accurately to keep people and businesses out of trouble!

The US tax system can be very complex. Dutiful citizens and businesses pay their fair share of tax obligations to support the well-being of society—they pay taxes on different levels, funding a variety of federal, state, and local services and programs, such as Social Security, Medicare, schools, and libraries. Income taxes serve as the largest source of revenue for the federal government, accounting for over 40 percent of annual tax revenue.

Tax accountancy offers accountants many different paths and opportunities. Many of the complex tax codes are now programmed into different types of tax software, and the role of tax accountants has evolved considerably. These accountants deliver insights regarding tax impacts to help businesses make better decisions. There are many areas of tax to specialize in, including individual tax, business tax, sales tax, and employment tax. Tax accountants can also work abroad with professional services firms.

Tax advisors play a crucial role in helping senior executives navigate the complex tax environment so they can focus on the business side of things. Many non-tax professionals are not savvy about taxes and, in most cases, are potentially overpaying for taxes. Every time the business or company spends money, it has a tax implication, and some are more significant than others. The structure of a deal may be the difference between potentially paying out a huge portion of profits or receiving benefits for the same action. For example, if a company buys another company, there is potential to both greatly increase or decrease that company's taxes as a result, all dependent on the structure of the purchase. Tax advisors help set up the purchase to maximize tax efficiency and thereby ensure company profit is as large as it can be. The areas we visited just now present merely a high-level overview of what a tax career could lead to. Let it be tax filing, planning, or strategy—it can be a really fun and challenging puzzle if you like people, numbers, and the law. The featured expert in this field, Jina Etienne, is creative, analytical, and an exceptional problem solver. Taxes are important and can be so much fun if you approach them as Jina does! Here, she shares how she kept an open mind as her career moved around like a Plinko game, trying different things, jumping through obstacles and challenges as they came, all the while adapting and learning. She took this concept further and applied this same rationale to people and diversity—after all, people matter, and everyone brings different skills and perspectives to the table. Diversity makes every problem much more fun and exciting to tackle!

11

Fearless Creation of Your Career Journey

Jina Etienne

TAX CONSULTANT, FORMER PRESIDENT OF
NABA (NATIONAL ASSOCIATION OF BLACK
ACCOUNTANTS), D&I CONSULTANT AND
#FEARLESSINCLUSION CHAMPION, AND SPEAKER

Jina's honest perspective is refreshing in the business world. She bravely tells you the core issues exactly as they are, nothing more, nothing less. Her effective communication skills are emboldened by her thoughtful, intentional listening and calm demeanor. I have heard her speak in several interviews and seminars, and each time I hear something enlightening and unique, presented candidly and straight to the point, which, frankly, is all too rare.

Jina is a diversity and inclusion (D&I) consultant. She came to this role through a series of career changes. She worked for a big firm after college, then ran her own accounting firm for more than 17 years. She sold her practice to join the American Institute of CPAs (AICPA), then left to become the president and CEO of the National Association of Black Accountants (NABA). After NABA, she joined Grant Thornton, one of the largest CPA firms in the US, as their director of diversity and inclusion. As a biracial woman, Jina cares deeply about D&I and coined the hashtag #FearlessInclusion as a representation of her passion, focus, and vision for what could be. She is not afraid to share her experiences of becoming more self-aware and developing the confidence to "be herself" at work.

Today, she aligns her consulting business with her passion and offers advice to organizations looking to build and create more inclusive cultures. Her goal is to help firms foster a sense of belonging to improve the employee experience and strengthen the connection between personal values, sense of purpose, and work.

I am confident and hopeful that with D&I advocates and champions like Jina, the accounting profession will be led toward greater innovation and creativity. Not just by improving diversity in the industry, but also through a deeper appreciation for the role of accountants within the work-place more generally. Rather than being viewed as number-crunching introverts, I hope we can become widely viewed and accepted as integral strategic decision-making partners for businesses.

Plinko

Remember the game Plinko on *The Price is Right*? You drop the chip in the top and it bounces randomly down to a slot at the bottom. Each slot has a different prize, and you don't know which box it might end up in, or what path it'll take to get there. That is how I feel about my career journey. In sixth grade, I decided I wanted to be an attorney. Then, in high school, my boyfriend's mother strengthened my resolve. She didn't know it, but she was a strong role model. She was an attorney, a great mother, and an all-around badass. Turns out, my university didn't offer an undergraduate pre-law major. I figured international business would be a good foundation for international law, so I chose to get a business degree. After struggling in a few classes, I started to worry that I might have made the wrong choice.

The business school required that students take accounting before declaring a major. Accounting sounded so boring, so I pushed it off until the last possible moment—second semester sophomore year. The class wasn't as boring as I expected or as hard as everyone described. I was surprised when I got an A. I went to talk to my professor afterward; I asked if all accounting classes were this easy. He laughed, then said no, and explained that accounting was one of those subjects where "either you get it or you don't." Apparently, I got it. When I told him I wanted to go to law school, he cheered the idea because the JD/CPA combination was great. At the time, I had no idea what a CPA was, but I changed my major anyway. He said it was a good thing and I trusted his advice. I grew excited about my future again. After taking a tax class at the start of my senior year, I got even more excited. Tax felt like a direct connection between the law and accounting. I was hooked! After graduation, I went straight into the tax department of an international accounting firm and never looked back. After passing the CPA exam, I went on to get a graduate degree in taxation.

My path taught me the importance of staying flexible, staying true to what you love, and utilizing the skills that come naturally to you. My brain liked problem-solving, creativity, and puzzles. I was also good at algebra, which is really just math that uses variables in solving equations and formulas. When accounting came easy and I could see how it fit in with my plans, I changed course. When I saw the connection between accounting and law, I pivoted again. After landing a prestigious job in a big firm, I knew specializing in tax felt like a natural fit, so I pursued an advanced degree. Just like Plinko, I bounced left, then right, then left again, and ended up winning the big prize—an amazing career! Throughout my career, I volunteered in my profession and the community. I wasn't afraid to put myself out there. That led to new opportunities and different roles with more and more influence across the profession. Volunteering on an AICPA committee led to my job as director of taxation. While there, I pivoted again to be more involved in conversations about diversity. Because I was able to demonstrate my strategic ability, the position led to my next role at NABA. If my story teaches you anything, it's this: don't stress if you don't know where you're going yet. Let your skills and passions guide you along the way like those bounces left and right on the Plinko board. And keep an open mind. Things don't often turn out the way you expect but, in my experience, they often end up where you were likely meant to be. Embrace the uncertainty of your future and be excited about the endless possibilities.

A Career in Tax Accountancy Can Be Many Things

When most people think of taxes, they think of tax returns. Sure, that's part of it, but there is so much more. First, there are a lot of different types of taxes: property tax, sales tax, gas tax, income tax, etc. Second, taxes are payments required by a federal, state, or local government. The requirements for those taxes come from a law or regulation.

The law determines:

- Who must pay the tax (i.e., corporation? individual? retailer?)
- What the tax is based on (i.e., income? property value? sales price?)
- How the tax is paid (i.e., included in the price of a product? withheld by a third party? filing a tax return?)
- When the tax is paid (i.e., on sale? quarterly? annually?)

Tax accountants must understand all of these rules so they can help businesses manage each of these factors. Tax accountants can work for a company (think: internal accounting department) or for a public accounting firm (most likely in the tax department). Tax work can be divided into 3 general areas: research, compliance, and planning. The research includes understanding law, monitoring court cases to understand how the law is interpreted and applied, looking for exceptions or alternatives, and keeping track of changes. Compliance is preparing tax returns and payment vouchers, as well as representing taxpayers before the IRS or state tax authorities. Tax planning is looking at income forecasts or projections and exploring different scenarios to either anticipate the tax that will be due (cash flow) or, possibly, do things differently to reduce the tax that will be due.

In my case, I worked in the tax department of a public accounting firm where I focused mostly on compliance, although I did my fair share of research and tax planning. I started my career in the tax department of Touche Ross (now Deloitte), where my job was mostly preparing tax returns for large corporations and doing tax research to support the positions being taken on tax returns. A position is just a fancy way of saying researching different options for how something could/should be taxed and then picking one—known as taking a "position."

I loved working there and learned a lot, but the culture and environment never felt like a "fit" for me. So, I decided to start my own practice. I worked mostly with small, startup businesses and expanded my services to include accounting and bookkeeping as well as business consulting. As an accountant and fellow entrepreneur (after all, I was also running a small business), I helped clients set up their new business, figure out how to run their business, and become accounting literate so they could learn to use their accounting information to evaluate operations, track growth, plan for taxes, and be more strategic in their decision-making and business planning.

I learned that I was a good teacher and could explain accounting in ways that made sense to non-accountants. I started to get invitations to speak to several small business groups and organizations. That led to opportunities to present at national accounting conferences and become a paid speaker at a national training company and an adjunct accounting professor at American University. By the time I sold my practice, I was spending the equivalent of 3 months a year speaking and training, as well as doing volunteer work at the state and national levels.

I sold my practice to become director of taxation for the AICPA. That job was focused on helping CPAs doing exactly what I had been doing when I was in practice. I was able to use my experience as a sole practitioner to develop technical resources, provide updates on changes to tax laws and regulations, and create practice guides to support small firm operations. I was also responsible for increasing awareness and understanding of IRS enforceable tax ethics rules, mostly through presentations and informational resources.

I loved tax because I was able to take advantage of my superpowers (that's what I call my natural strengths and skills). In my case, those were creativity, strategy, problem-solving, and analytical thinking. That combination of skills worked perfectly for tax because I understood the law, how it related to accounting transactions, and how it then translated into the numbers used on tax returns. It felt like finding the optimal factors to use (tax planning) in a giant algebraic equation (tax compliance) to get the best result for the client (lowest tax paid). Sure, we filled out forms, but that's the end product of a process where each box requires thinking, analysis, research, and a little creativity. It requires an understanding of current tax law, entity structure, and accounting results. We need to choose what information goes on which forms, know what the consequences for tax will be, and communicate in effective ways with our clients. Successful tax accountants also need to be able to talk beyond the process. Project management and relationship building with clients is just as important as the technical work. If your brain likes doing analysis, creative planning, and puzzles, this is a great field to enter.

Creating My Place When None Could Be Found

Outwardly, I appear Black, but jokingly call myself an "other." I am biracial. My mother is Filipina, and my father is Black. I also grew up in a city like no other—Columbia, Maryland, established on June 21, 1967. I was just 2 months old at the time. Columbia was founded by James Rouse with a vision of a multicultural, interfaith community. I grew up in a fully integrated community with neighbors and classmates from a mix of races, religions, and ethnicities. There were also a few non-traditional families on my street, including a family with 2 adopted children and a lesbian couple, both of which were the kind of differences people didn't talk about openly back in the day. In my early 20s, I learned that my parents, just like in *The Loving Story* movie, had to get married in Washington, DC, because interracial marriage was illegal in Maryland at the time. They lived in Baltimore in a neighborhood friendly to an interracial couple, then moved to Columbia shortly after it was founded. They wanted to establish a family home in a place where they could raise a family where they were accepted as equal members of the community. Columbia quickly grew, exceeding Rouse's development and cultural goals. Today, it is still very diverse and has consistently ranked as one of the best places to live in America.

Looking back, I'm eternally grateful that they took a chance on a new city, with untested social, religious, and cultural norms. I grew up in a place where I wasn't defined by my race, gender, or religion. I grew up with the belief that I wasn't limited by race or gender. It gave me the confidence to try new things, explore new ideas, and brave through whatever uncertainty was in front of me.

In college, I quickly learned that the rest of the world didn't view me the same way. I went to a predominantly White college where I was quickly labeled as "Black." Although I was given the opportunity to attend an incredible school, my race seemed to limit my social options. I was accepted in class, but never quite felt like I fit in at the student lounge. After graduation, that feeling persisted. I never felt like I fit in at work. That is a big reason I decided to start my own firm. I didn't think I could find a place where I would naturally fit in, so I created my own firm. At first, I tried to look like every other firm, because I thought I'd need to prove I was like every other accountant to get clients. Over time, I learned that authenticity was the foundation of a strong, long-lasting client relationship. They weren't trusting some generic accountant; they were trusting *me*! Once I stopped trying to be what I thought I should be, my business grew. After that, I never

THE WORLD OF TAXATION

had to do any marketing. All of my business was through referral, and we grew every year. In fact, the size of my practice doubled for 2 consecutive years. At my largest, I had 5 employees, but I never felt like I was running a firm.

My practice taught me the importance of being yourself and building authentic relationships. I am grateful for being able to carve out a sector of the accounting industry that was just my own and work with people who could see this vision alongside me. I was doing something that I was good at (accounting), for people who appreciated me (my clients), and with a great team (my employees). When you love your job, it never feels like work!

Diversity Is More Than Different People Working Together

After a few years in practice, I started volunteering. First, for a local nonprofit that offers tax preparation and representation services for low-income taxpayers in Washington, DC, then for the Maryland Association of CPAs, and eventually at the AICPA. Volunteer service helped build my confidence as fellow CPA volunteers validated my view and perspectives around client service, employee engagement, business operations, and firm structure. While a volunteer at the AICPA, I met Jim Metzler, a vice president responsible for small firm services. He was the first person who saw something in me that I did not see in myself professionally, which sparked me to try to move outside of my comfort zone. Over the years, he has been a great mentor, advocate, and champion. He taught me that good leaders listen well and create safe spaces for their team. He let me think out loud, helped validate my thinking, asked questions to clarify his understanding of my intention, never expected me to filter what I said, and really helped me see that my perspectives were different, valuable, and worth sharing with others.

Sharing my perspectives, challenging the status quo, brainstorming new or different ways to do things, and always raising my hand to help became big parts of my professional brand. It opened doors to new opportunities, first internally helping other teams besides my own, and eventually to a new role as the CEO of NABA. It was the move that first gave me permission to agitate, challenge, and champion for others. I felt like I was in a position to say things that others either may not want to say or may not feel safe sharing. I had an obligation to ask tough questions and push on behalf of so many groups that still struggle with underrepresentation, access, permission, and empowerment.

I've come to view the word "diversity" as distracting. It focuses on identity politics and seems to define inclusion as a measure of how comfortable minorities feel in predominantly White workplaces. A culture of inclusivity is one where those differences are not only respected but valued for the unique perspectives that they bring. I believe there is more work to be done. Inclusion is the intention of those in the majority and how they want those in the minority to feel comfortable in their space. I believe we need to shift the conversation and strive for multicultural workplaces where everyone belongs and is appreciated regardless of differences. Safe spaces, where every member of the community feels safe to be their authentic selves, are inherently more productive. This is true for White men, too. Diversity has to be true for all of us, and so far, the diversity conversation tends to exclude White men. They need to be included so that we can talk about diversity holistically and get beyond the superficial. The visible stuff is easy. It's the invisible stuff that's hard, and we have more invisible stuff than we have visible stuff.

As a biracial woman who never felt like I fit in anywhere, I've experienced moments throughout my career when I felt like an outsider, so I held back. It didn't feel safe to speak my mind or express my view. I don't want anyone to feel that way anymore. Today, I work hard to help organizations foster cultures of belonging—when someone can be their unique, quirky, different self and still get invited to happy hour. I share my experiences, both good and bad, to help others connect, express, and overcome the challenges of exclusion. The struggle with authenticity is real. Corporate culture is fairly conservative and doesn't have a great history of supporting those who speak up or show up differently than the traditional norms, styles, and behaviors of that company's culture. The fears and anxieties of bringing your whole self to work in corporate America are real. In the early days of my career, I made the mistake of ignoring my inner voice and chose a job that looked fantastic on paper but turned out to be a horrible fit for me. I had to put in a lot of effort covering myself so that I could show up like everyone else.

Today, businesses are finally starting to understand the importance of diversity, equity, and inclusion. Many have fully developed D&I strategies, while others built initiatives targeting specific areas of their process, culture, or business norms. I encourage everyone to ask potential employers about D&I: Do you have a D&I strategy? Do you have employee resource groups? What activities do you engage in that demonstrate your commitment to diversity? Don't be afraid to ask questions about company culture to truly grasp the extent to which they value and support their stated D&I commitment and goals. Seek transparency in what they are actively doing to build and create an inclusive culture. If they are unwilling to share, that might be a sign that their commitment isn't as strong.

Crucially, what the company is doing to ensure the culture is inclusive is secondary to what you are personally doing every day to show up as an inclusive member of the company. Today, partners in CPA firms are still predominantly White and male. On the bright side, more women and minorities are pursuing accounting degrees, and staff below the manager level in CPA firms is more diverse than ever before. More firms are committed to diversity and inclusion. Give the profession a chance. Diversity at the top is just a matter of time.

Management Information Systems

Advancement in technology and information systems has transformed not only the accounting profession itself but also the way accountants work. The way we count, calculate, record, and keep track of different transactions has definitely come a long way since ancient times, which used pebbles and abacuses. Through the calculator, we have advanced to the modern era, where we are heavily reliant on electronic spreadsheets. In today's cloud-based era, business growth is accelerated continually by countless innovative and creative cloud-based systems, from mobile apps to artificial intelligence (AI) systems. These new methods are far more accessible to businesses as they require fewer technical departments and teams.

Accountants in many cases have become the administrators or managers of enterprise resource planning (ERP) systems, instead of relying heavily on the IT department. In an ERP system, the solution is a single integrated system for the entire company. These integrated ERPs support internal functions such as finance, accounting, inventory control, and much more.

With the rise of the internet and cloud-based services, there has been a rise in the Software-as-a-Service (SaaS) business model. SaaS is a software distribution model that is used when applications are hosted by a third-party provider over the internet. In other words, instead of having to buy and install software on the users' computers, users pay a monthly subscription to the SaaS provider and store everything in the cloud.

Working through technology rather than around it allows for accountants to create operational efficiencies. At the same time, however, there are numerous cybersecurity risks associated with SaaS. Interruptions due to IT security breaches affect daily business operations, a company's reputation, and customer trust. To protect against these risks, SaaS systems are expected to have built-in controls that must be in compliance with the internal controls requirements. These controls can take many forms, including limited access for different levels of users, password restrictions, and review and approval requirements.

Companies are highly aware of the importance of ensuring proper security protocols are being followed and of protecting the privacy and confidentiality of their users' data. Any exam or audit generally starts off with a comprehensive questionnaire to get a sense of the current state of the particular system by identifying key risks and controls. What are the security measures to prohibit someone from violating/hacking into the system? Where is the backup data stored? What is the protocol in case an unexpected event occurs? To pass the audit, companies must have adequate answers to questions such as these.

System automation has helped make almost all accounting processes more efficient. Systems provide accountants with a way to build and enhance different reports easily, leading to a more effective method of interpreting data, thus making the work of an accountant much easier. The role of the accountant has shifted in proportion to these raised expectations—rather than being in charge of numbers, accountants think critically about the strategic steps forward, moving their roles from purely "keeping the books" to becoming trusted business advisors.

Senior executives, business strategists, and operational leaders always push for a higher "single source of truth" in business—a centralized system that they can rely on to get accurate insights for accounting and business activities at their fingertips. There are many robust systems in the market, not only to keep track of client information and data but also to control all of the backup supporting documents and sources such as invoices, contracts, and agreements. There are a lot of unique systems that are built for specific purposes. Accounting software, for example, automates an organization's financial functions and transactions with modules such as accounts payable and receivable, payroll, and billing.

When a company grows, it likely outgrows its previous system and will need to either upgrade its existing system or switch to a completely new one. If companies merge together, they need to reevaluate their legacy system to see if it still affords future growth. System projects such as these (system implementation, system conversion) are commonly included in the job specifications for controllers. At a more junior level, accountants can participate in these projects as well.

As demonstrated in the stories of Kimberly Ellison-Taylor and Michael Whitmire, knowing and understanding the systems that you may encounter—and the opportunities they afford for growth—can only improve your standing as an accountant and valuable member of any company.

Maybe one day you will create a better and smarter system than what we have today!

12

Serendipity in Accounting and Technology

Kimberly N. Ellison-Taylor

GLOBAL TECHNOLOGY AND FINANCE
EXECUTIVE AT ORACLE AND FORMER CHAIRMAN
OF AMERICAN INSTITUTE OF CPAS

Kimberly's energy is contagious. She's probably one of the few people who was excited about the prospect of becoming a CPA when she was only 8 years old! Kimberly rose through the ranks of the accounting profession with an intense focus on technology, spurred by a determination to get out of her hometown and be successful. By stumbling upon information technology in college, Kimberly uniquely set herself up to be a powerful leader in a business world that has become increasingly reliant on technology, without even realizing it.

Incredibly, Kimberly is the youngest person, the fifth woman, and the first person of color to serve as the chairman of the American Institute of CPAs since the organization's founding 133 years ago. As a leader, she promoted not only the accounting profession itself but also next-generation leadership, technology, and an increase in representation and leadership among women and minorities more generally.

Today, Kimberly is a transformational strategic leader who has had a compelling career in finance and technology. She is currently leading finance thought leadership at Oracle, one of the global tech giants. Over the years, she has spearheaded many different strategies and innovations in the accounting and finance profession, using her extensive knowledge and experience in both fields.

I admire Kimberly's strength. She is an example of a strong role model for women determined to defy the odds. Coming from humble beginnings, she recognized the importance of feeling a sense of belonging, reaching out to people, and building a community to help serve others. She is heavily involved in her community, helping the less fortunate, and often mentors young people in her community and workplace. Her goal is to bring awareness of the many opportunities within accounting to the next generation. As a frequent keynote speaker on technology topics, inclusive leadership, and the next generation of finance talent, Kimberly is helping to represent others who might not have a strong voice, and opening the door for their entrance to the accounting field more broadly. It is the legacy and impact that motivates her to constantly do more in the profession for our next generation of finance and technology leaders.

Don't Change the Goal in Response to a Challenge. Change the Plan.

The first time I took the CPA exam, I failed. I was extremely disappointed. I didn't put in enough time, effort, and energy. I was way too comfortable with my ability to study alone. After all, I graduated valedictorian and went to college on a full scholarship.

Although it seemed like the end of the world at the time, failing the CPA exam taught me an important lesson: to focus and prioritize in order to follow my dreams. I didn't give up on my dream of being a CPA. I changed my approach—I needed a strategy and an undivided focus; I needed to actually listen and follow the advice from the older group of people who had already done it and succeeded. The failure opened my eyes to the importance of learning from others and paying attention to lessons learned.

Practice and preparation are the keys to unlocking success. I had to fail the exam to realize this; my failure, however, strengthened my resolve and dedication to succeed. I signed up for a review course, completed practice tests for months, retook the exam that November, and passed! I dedicated months of blood, sweat, and tears, and my hard work paid off. I make every single day *worth it*. I internalize the power of growth and success through failure, and share my lessons learned to motivate others. It's been such a huge return on that time investment over and over again. That's what I tell my sons when I am talking with them about the importance of accounting and how accountants speak the language of business.

I Wanted to Be a CPA When I Grew Up!

I grew up in the inner city of Baltimore and I lived across the street from a library.

My mom instilled a love of reading in me from a young age, and through reading, I imagined a world of endless possibilities.

My dad worked rotating hours at Bethlehem Steel, a factory in Baltimore, and had never taken a sick day, despite having a long daily commute using 2 buses. My mom was a stay-at-home mom who took great care of me and my sisters while my dad worked. Through them, I learned the importance of being a lifelong learner and a hard worker.

I remember being in third grade, at a career day event, listening to the discussion about lawyers, doctors, and engineers. All those cool professions seemed interesting, but only when CPAs came up did it finally click. I wanted to learn how to manage money and have an impact. I could be the boss. I got excited thinking about managing money, having a CPA degree, a TV in every room in the house, a car, and even endless, sweet cereal!

Serendipity in Accounting and Technology

With my heart in accounting, however, I asked the wrong question when I went to college at the University of Maryland Baltimore County. "Can I be a CPA after I finish here?" They said yes. Later on, I found out that I would need to major in economics. I didn't want to do that.

After reviewing my other options for a major, I enrolled in an information technology management major. After that degree, I went on to earn an MBA. I still wanted to be a CPA, though, so I went to community college at night to get an accounting certificate while working at the National Aeronautics and Space Administration (NASA). Little did I know at the time that my career would heavily cross over between the 2 worlds—accounting and technology—and would lead to me pursuing a great career at the intersection of both.

We are accountants, sure, but we use technology to do accounting. Clients look to us as advisors and place trust in our knowledge and use of technological advancements. Technology enables dramatic shifts in business models, ways of delivering services, and the accounting industry itself. As technology evolves, worldwide collaborations become seamless, clients' expectations change, and our solutions continue to advance. It's worthwhile to invest time to learn and stay abreast of the latest developments by reading, researching, and talking to others. It'll arm you with the tools you need to succeed.

Your Passions and Interests Will Light the Path toward Your Career

I believe there are endless possibilities within accounting. It is a foundational skillset, and getting a CPA is instrumental in any industry: healthcare, audit, manufacturing, tax, entertainment, sports, and the list goes on. I was able to combine both of my heart's desires: accounting and technology.

For me, developing critical thinking allowed me to succeed in technology and accounting. Critical thinking in analyzing transactions and assimilating data is incredibly similar to that of programming in the technology world, so I focused on honing this skillset. I didn't have a vision for this when I started in college, but I found my purpose through action and mentors.

If you aren't yet sure where your interests lie, focus on what you like and where you can make a difference. Make it your career. It will serve you well.

Bring Your Authentic Self to Work Every Day

I have always been heavily involved in accounting organizations to promote the accounting profession to diverse individuals. I firmly believe that everyone, regardless of background, should be able to see themselves in this role. It would be terrible if a little Black girl didn't think she could become a CPA because she didn't see Black accountants as role models.

In order to do my part in bringing my awareness of the uncommon talent that exists in uncommon places, I offer my experiences to motivate and inspire others. Everyone has a voice that matters. Especially heartwarming to me are the emails, posts, and letters that I've gotten from people all over the world saying, "I never thought I'd see the day that there was a Black chairman at AICPA, a woman at that." I am hopeful that they realize that they too can achieve amazing things.

I often encourage young professionals to look for employers that enable them to be their best selves and pave the way for others. There's always room at the table. Help pull up a chair.

13

Mission Incredible

*Building a Best-in-Class System for
Accountants by Accountants*

Michael Whitmire

FOUNDER AND CEO OF FLOQAST,
AUTHOR, AND PODCAST HOST

Michael is the co-founder of FloQast, one of the fastest-growing venture capital-backed companies. FloQast was founded in 2013. With 3 rounds of funding raising nearly $100 million, the company has established its place in the market while building partnerships and relationships in the marketplace.

The accounting community has noticed the disruption of this incredible company. All accountants know how tedious the month-end close process can be. The most crucial part is to ensure that all the numbers are accurately recorded, and the process requires late-night hours near tight deadlines. Most people take this part of the job for granted, recognizing that was just part of the accountants' job to meet tight deadlines. Thankfully, the CEO and founder of FloQast, Michael Whitmire, isn't like most people. He was able to see challenges as opportunities. While experiencing the numerous inefficiencies firsthand as an accountant, he decided that there could (and should) be a better way! So, he created FloQast. While running and building his company, Michael continued to be heavily involved in mentoring the younger generations of accountants. His book, Controller's Code: The Secret Formula to a Successful Career in Finance, *and podcast,* Blood, Sweat and Balance Sheets, *touch on the many core technical and leadership aspects that most accountants face and may struggle with throughout their career path to becoming controllers and CFOs. Michael's journey and inspiration gives me tremendous hope for young professionals and our next generations of accountants.*

Discover My Own Venture

I have always held an entrepreneurial spirit. Growing up in Los Angeles, I navigated my childhood by creating and discovering new ventures wherever they could be found. Like many children, I started with a lemonade stand. My mom participated in these ventures, covering expenses and allowing me to keep the revenue. I had a sweet deal going. My parents are both entrepreneurs; my mother was the president of a Los Angeles real estate company before she started her own consulting firm. Their ambitions and companies were inspirational; they normalized entrepreneurship. My dad, a partner at a law firm, also created his own business. My family dynamics created an ideal environment for an entrepreneurial mind to develop.

I went into college to study film. In my second semester, I realized that I was more interested in pursuing business. I started taking different classes and quickly realized that I was good at accounting. I still remember how great I felt the first time I completed a journal entry exercise that tied out the trial balance. I decided that my career would start in the world of accounting. I would do it for a little while until I was able to start my own company. Turns out, working in a company was the best way to start to learn how to build one.

The More You Work, the More You Learn

I always wanted to ring the bell that signified a company would be traded publicly on the stock market. I wanted to help bring a company to its IPO, and I wanted to bring my own company to its IPO. I didn't realize that I would get access to these opportunities as soon as I did.

During my junior year, I received a job offer to work at Ernst & Young in Los Angeles. I used the opportunity to gain as much knowledge about the industry as possible. I ended up being with EY for 3.5 years, working within the entertainment group to audit film and record label companies. The opportunity was great, but I was ready to move on to something new.

At EY, if someone said a job was going to be a good learning experience, it meant you would be working a ton. I recognize that learning requires hard work. The negativity associated with a good learning experience is quite disheartening—the reality of the situation is the more you work, the more you learn. It almost always pays off in the end. Take on the complicated job where you need to figure things out and learn. It will positively impact your career.

Cornerstone hired me as employee 95. They were a year out from their IPO when they recruited me, and I was overwhelmed with excitement. I worked there for 13 months and brought the company public. Along the way, though, I became burned out, felt that I wasn't receiving adequate support from the company, and just didn't think the position was worth my time. I quit and started down the entrepreneurial journey. I started a fantasy gambling website with some friends. Cornerstone signed me on again, 3 months later, for a short-term assignment that ended up lasting 18 months. I had a totally new role, and I loved it. I worked as a consultant, helping with new projects. I led Cornerstone through all of the SOX compliance and adoptions. I helped document the entire risk and control matrix and implement new policies and procedures. It was certainly not what I was expecting, but I was learning and loving the experience every day.

One day, the VP of finance explained to me a situation that Cornerstone found itself in. They had acquired a company from New Zealand without doing any due diligence on the company's financial standing. The VP asked for my help. "Can you audit the company, convert the company's numbers to GAAP, integrate the information with our already existing system, get the operations running, and then get someone to take over for you?" Yes! I mean, how could I say no to such an opportunity? If I had anything to learn from my experiences thus far, it was that taking on more work would only lead to higher levels of learning. I grew excited at the possibilities that lay before me.

The New Zealand company was an SaaS company, and since I had to go back in time 3 years to audit all 3 contracts, I was basically rebuilding their financials from scratch. As a 3-year-old SaaS company, their recurring revenue business model was successfully established. The specific acquisition project at Cornerstone, my last work for the company, gave me both the idea and confidence to follow through with creating my own company, FloQast.

I stepped away from Cornerstone initially because I was uninspired and burnt out. When I returned, with a new position, I felt invigorated. Saying yes to consulting, while more work, meant more learning. I loved the opportunity to roll up my sleeves and get my hands dirty with new opportunities. I always say yes to actions that inspire me, which ensures that I enter my office excited each morning. That the New Zealand opportunity fell into my lap only solidified my desire to work harder and smarter on the things that inspired me.

Frustrating Realities Can Be Changed

FloQast was born out of frustration. I identified a problem that most accountants struggle through: the month-end. I often describe the month close process as "death by a thousand papercuts." The minutiae connected with solving these often increase the time and effort required to finish them tenfold. I created software, by accountants for accountants, that we could sell as a service and market as a unique way of efficiently completing the month-end program. There is no one pain point that our service fixed; rather, it worked through multiple. Standardizing your processes, getting everything organized, communicating and collaborating as a team, getting through checklists, automating reconciliations, preparing you for the audit, documenting review notes, etc.

When I left Cornerstone, all I had was a vision and some irrational confidence. I believed that no matter what, with my resources, I would be able to create my own adventure. I used *cofounderslab.com*—basically a dating website for entrepreneurs—and met with over 60 engineers. Eventually, I connected with our current engineer, and he became the second co-founder. A friend of mine that I went to college with joined as a third co-founder. The 3 of us, newly labeled co-founders, started searching for ways to raise money.

It was hard to find initial investors for our new technology company. Explaining the problem that our service solved to non-accountants was especially difficult. I found it nearly impossible to explain concisely how difficult a month-end close is. One of the first investors that we had lined up for the project pulled their investment out while I was on my flight to their office! Since the stock market's numbers plummeted, the investors decided to pull the investment—entirely disregarding our verbal agreement.

I felt defeated, frustrated, and ethically cheated by the investors and the market. I was so close! I continued to search for investors. The market took a few months to turn around, and we eventually secured funding with higher-quality investors with expertise, at a higher valuation. After numerous nos, we finally got an introduction to Toba Capital. Now, 7 years later, we have raised $93 million, built a company with 200 amazing people, partnered with incredible founders, and found investors who align with our vision.

Transparency Is the Key.
The Company Goal Is the Lock.
With the Two, You'll Unlock the Future.

Once the business took off, and the market proved that the problem we were solving existed, the landscape of fundraising changed dramatically. We had a name out there; the conversations became less about pitching the necessity of our project and more toward understanding the soundness of our business. I found it a lot more natural at that point to communicate our intention and reach that coveted yes.

Growing our business took time and effort, and I knew that the company I was creating needed a culture that would keep employees happy, connected, and involved. My mission statements included transparent company culture, making accountants' lives easier, and becoming an anchor SaaS company in the Los Angeles ecosystem.

I am inspired in having built a company my younger self would have wanted to work for. Millennials like to be in the know. They want to be involved as much as they can. Oftentimes, they want a deeper under-standing of company history, current plans, and future goals. I am happy to have created a culture surrounded by this idea: I keep employ-ees informed on their potential career paths and promotions within the company while being completely transparent about new hires. This creates a more engaging work environment, where employees feel like they are a part of the business at the structural level. I hope to go public and become known in the general sphere to help the city, accountants, and my employees thrive.

Celebrating Numerical Knowledge + Debunking Accountant Stereotypes

The only main difference between the general population and accoun-tants is that accountants understand a bit more about numbers, tax returns, and financial statements! This knowledge should be cele-brated, not mocked!

I work with and around accountants all day: they are my friends, employees, and clients. I have met thousands of accountants over the years, and my relationship with the profession positions me to call out the inaccuracies surrounding the accounting stereotype. Accountants are not boring, static, or monotonous. There are all kinds of accountants: cool, nerdy, sporty, etc. Since accountants are incredibly accustomed to being ripped on, we understand the stereotypes and embrace them—we are more comfortable in our own skin than most other people. Sprinkle in some self-deprecating humor, sarcasm, and nerdy hobbies, and you've created a more accurate portrait of the accountant.

Another stereotype about accountants is that they can't sell; I find that this is blatantly false. Our sales team is full of accountants who are confident, good communicators who know the art of selling and have learned how to work a sales process—salespeople who really want to close business. These people are accountants and non-accountants alike! Interestingly, at FloQast, the success rate in sales is much higher for accountants than non-accountants. In fact, half of my sales team are accountants!

The field of accounting provides an incredible learning opportunity. For one to be a successful financial executive, one must have a concrete understanding of the stories that numbers tell. Accounting requires using numbers to influence business decisions; being able to apply the concept of the story within the numbers is incredibly powerful. Accountants have access to information that almost no one else at a company is privy to—being able to dig into financial statements and build stories out of numbers will truly teach you so much about how to start, build, and run a company.

If starting your own company is what you are interested in, take advantage of your time in audit and your time in accounting: use that information to learn how to do the processes. You will one day need it for your own company!

Sales And Marketing

As a young professional, I had mixed feelings about sales and marketing. I found marketing creatives to be very interesting, but I did not fully understand their work. Since the marketing profession is very ideas-based, I struggled to grasp the importance and substance of their work. It was all so different from my analytical accounting background. Their methods were confusing, and I initially felt as though their work contained very little substantive value.

Gradually, I began to understand why there existed such a wide disconnect between my understanding and that of my marketing peers. We both work to present information in different ways. Accountants are trained to be rational, logical, and analytical. The vast majority of what we do is based solely on concrete facts and numbers. Marketing creatives, in contrast, use storytelling to explain the core message behind the facts, and through that, elevate their brand and connect to customers.

As I grew in the professional field, I continued to research and understand the importance of marketing on an individual and business level. I learned the importance of communicating to clients the core tenets of yourself and telling the story of your services. You have to answer the questions about who you are. Are you an expert? In what field? Are you a problem solver? How do you communicate that to others?

I found that accountants, my younger self included, lacked the skills to market themselves. I remember being fresh out of college and constantly bombarded with advice to put myself out there, network, meet recruiters, and market myself as an intelligent hard worker. I found the advice frustrating and even annoying. What did it all even mean?

I knew that my work was great, but I didn't understand why I had to present my case to others. I only fully understood the value of marketing when someone presented it to me in the context of differentiating myself from the crowd. Since there exists a ton of top talent in the accounting world, I needed to find a way to stand out. When everyone graduates from top-notch schools, how could I effectively compete with others? Turns out, marketing was the solution.

Of course, marketing also plays a major role in the success of businesses and their projects. No matter what product or service one sells, they have to connect with their customers and present the case of how their product or service provides the value they are looking for. Importantly, this is not always the value that you see in the object.

For example, let's say my new career is as a car salesman. I think the best thing about having a car is being able to get around conveniently; my clients, however, believe that having a car represents a portion of their identity and may even determine if they warrant a high-class status. Selling the car would require me to understand and adapt to this target audience, and I would do so by explaining how the car would elevate their status and identity—a feat that many car commercials accomplish within the first 15 seconds. At the same time, I would also provide the client with my own point of view on the incredible convenience of the car, all the while attempting to reach them on a personal and emotional level. Many times, buying something or closing a deal in business is the result of mostly emotional and psychological processes and relatively less analytical power. As a result, marketing is heavily rooted in stories, which usually have emotional undertones and connections.

You may ask, then, how do you know what your customers want? By constantly learning the various types of products out there in the market and talking to customers to gain an understanding of their needs. In this, networking and communication are key. The conversation can get really interesting when your knowledge is broad, has variety, and connects to a global reach. Depending on your audience, you may benefit from bringing in experiences about driving a car, carpooling, or even your best friend who enjoyed racing cars. The more you know your market and audiences, the more intuitively this instinct will come. This instinct becomes one of the most powerful tools that most salespeople have.

Importantly, Andrew Moses shows that you can leverage your accounting skills and experiences to transition into the sales and marketing field. Although it may not be an easy, smooth, or natural transition, it can be done, as you will read in Andrew's story.

Andrew's story shares with us the essential skills that helped his progression in his career, through marketing and business development. He has a strong foundation in accounting, which he is able to combine with his creativity to connect and build trust with his clients, ultimately delivering innovative solutions and building a broader network in the world of growing startups.

14

Master Connector Optimizing the Power of Networking

Andrew Moses

BUSINESS DEVELOPMENT AND MARKETING EXECUTIVE
AT MORGANFRANKLIN CONSULTING, PODCAST
HOST, AND ADJUNCT MARKETING PROFESSOR

Andrew is an effective marketing leader, master connector, and networker. He brings the best events in town! I was honored to be invited to one of his signature networking events in New York City, which he created several years ago with the goal of bringing growth-oriented companies together for accounting and finance professionals to network and share knowledge. Whenever I find the time to step away from the chaos of work to attend a social or networking event, I have the best experience. Hanging out with fellow professionals, talking about all things business and personal. Meeting new friends and reconnecting with old ones is always quite fun. Some of us ended up being great friends and even hired each other!

Aside from being the vice president of business development and marketing at MorganFranklin Consulting, Vaco's global consulting firm, Andrew is constantly proactively taking on challenging opportunities to help others, from building a marketing curriculum to teach a college class of 70 people last-minute, to raising money through "Autism Speaks U," an autism research and awareness program that he founded. Most recently, Andrew's podcast, Everybody Pulls the Tarp, *has gained a lot of traction from business leaders and professionals from all walks of life.*

Andrew's story is a great reminder that starting your career in account-ing does not necessarily mean finishing it there: your personal abilities can take you in many directions until you find the best fit. Understanding how clients and accountants think, being able to see things from multiple per-spectives, and knowing how to communicate with clients are key skills that will be applicable if you switch to another field down the road. The expe-riences you will gain from studying accounting and working in finance can be used as stepping stones to a personally fulfilling career in creativity, marketing, or, ultimately, anything you find interesting!

Accounting as the Stepping Stone

Like many high school and college students, I was not sure what I wanted to be when I grew up. I knew that I was interested in busi-ness, but I didn't think accounting was for me. However, after an internship in the front office of the Trenton Thunder, the AA affiliate of the New York Yankees, I decided to major in accounting. Starting my career in accounting felt like a great way to build a foundation—after all, finance and accounting are the backbones of any business.

I graduated from Penn State's Smeal College of Business and, like many others starting out in the profession, interned, and then worked as an audit associate at KPMG. Candidly, I did not enjoy the work, but it was a necessary step to get to where I wanted to go. I decided to view it as a medical residency that I just needed to get through. My grandfather, who escaped Nazi Germany and created a successful manufacturing business, inspired my work ethic and focus on not taking things for granted. I had to keep moving forward with a positive perspective, remembering that my current reality could always be worse.

Look Forward with Intention

The economic downturn in 2008 hit everyone and every industry hard, including the accounting industry. I lost my job at KPMG. Despite having minimal interest in the job, I was hurt when all of a sudden, my control was taken away. This huge obstacle, and a depressed economy, forked a wedge in my career path. No longer could I depend on my employer to ensure I would be successful. I had to depend on myself.

I found value in looking forward with intention. This transition period, for me, provided a place for introspective reflection to deeply think about what I wanted to do. I knew that sitting back in my chair, finding a position, and being comfortable would never truly suit my intellectual desire to pursue an influential career. My layoff freed me to truly rethink my aspirations; I finally decided that I wanted to do something in a broader professional services capacity, as opposed to just audit or tax. My desire led me to look for positions that were more advisory in nature. They were roles where I would have a lot of opportunities to interact with my clients and cultivate relationships. I wanted to identify opportunities for improvement and create solutions, not simply find them and leave them to others to resolve.

After a lot of googling, I stumbled upon MorganFranklin Consulting. Of the 3 founders, 2 were also alumni of Penn State, and it was a unique company. It was a compilation of former Big 4 auditors, industry accountants, finance professionals, and technology consultants. They were not doing audits or tax prep; the firm was truly "non-conflicted" as it relates to the professional services industry and took on relevant finance, technology, and business advisory work to support its clients. It was a perfect fit. I'm not sure where I would be today without my layoff. It pushed me to look for opportunities with intention, and find deeper meaning and fulfillment that money, status, or power never can fill.

My wife and I have 2 daughters. The 3 of them mean the world to me. I enjoy my work but it's important for me to organize myself and my time so that I serve the needs of all stakeholders in my life, including my family. Overall, I compartmentalize my goals into 12-week time intervals, recognizing that the average person can accomplish 3 major tasks a day. I always have a few big quarterly goals and small daily goals to reach for when I wake up in the morning. I align my schedule so that I can accomplish the tasks that take the most time and capacity in my golden hours of work, which are different for everyone. For me, those hours are early in the morning. I also use this app called Todoist to keep track of tasks and effectively complete my goals on time! Life can be hectic but finding your ideal time to work and building a daily schedule around that, with long-term semesterly goals interspersed, is a great way to ensure efficiency, productivity, and purpose in your everyday actions and work.

Everybody Pulls the Tarp

I walked into the first day of my internship in minor league baseball expecting to be placed behind a desk and learn the business of sports. One hour in and the team's general manager tells me that I'd have to help the grounds crew pull the tarp on and off the field when it rains. Turns out, minor league organizations typically have smaller grounds crews than their major league counterparts and everyone, from the CEO to the new interns, pitched in to help ensure that the field could be covered properly. I rolled up my sleeves and pulled the tarp alongside members from every level of the organization. Pulling the tarp reinforced in me the idea that everyone needs to pitch in, regardless of what their title is. I pulled the tarp side-by-side with the team's CEO and individuals from every department in the organization. By pulling the tarp, we each acknowledged that there was no task above or beneath us. We were there to support the team and do whatever it took to ensure they were successful.

I believe in the power of cooperation and teamwork beyond one's expected roles and job descriptions. Recently, I've taken this belief and used it as the foundational philosophy for a new podcast, *Everybody Pulls the Tarp*. Each week, I interview Olympians, professional athletes, elite coaches, CEOs, bestselling authors, and other inspirational people about leadership, work ethic, and career development. I find value and lessons in each of their stories and feel honored to be able to share these lessons with others so that they can learn.

If you're a young professional, I urge you to step beyond your outlined duties and contribute to your team in meaningful, well-rounded ways that will help grow the entire company upward. Think not of what precisely your job title requests of you, but of what you bring to the table, and how you can leverage your abilities to cooperate and collaborate in meaningful ways.

The Importance of Relationships

Keith Ferrazzi said it best: never eat alone. In his book, *Never Eat Alone,* which I recommend to almost anyone I come across, Keith explains a theory of relationship-building that sees the potential for earned value through giving. Relationships, he argues, are key to success in one's career; spending time (for example, by sharing a meal) with another person is an incredibly effective way of building relationships. Once you have laid the foundation for an effective friendship, brainstorm ways that you can potentially give to the other. Did you recently read an article that you think they would enjoy? Is your college-age friend a perfect match for their new internship program? Can you think of any points of connection in your network that you could point them toward that could help them through a problem you discussed?

I always focus my relationships on giving first. Mutual benefit is the key to successful relationships, friendships, and mentorships. Mentorship is a 2-way street. I learn both as a mentee and as a mentor. As a mentor, I learn from engaging with my mentees in valuable ways. This level of connection results in a special relationship, where the mentor becomes invested in your success, learns from your critical thinking, and guides you toward success. I find that an authentic mentorship pairing is one in which both parties are confident in their power and ability to provide for the other. If you're a young professional, or college student, or just looking for a mentor, don't be afraid to ask those who inspire you. They do not view these tasks as burdens. In fact, it's quite the opposite! Most mentors, myself included, are eager to help open the door behind them, advising against their past mistakes to prevent others from following in those messy footsteps. While I understand trepidation or fear in approaching more experienced individuals, everyone has an opportunity to ask for guidance. Be intentional and specific with your questions, ask for advice, and keep reaching out. The best relationships will develop authentically based on shared interests, so be confident in what you value and seek, and keep asking others for help. Seriously, go try it out. Get on LinkedIn and message 3 people right now. Hey, if you don't know where to start, reach out to me on LinkedIn! Ask potential mentors about the most fulfilling part of their career, or things they wish they knew about their position before going into it. Ask for a Zoom call to chat a bit about their career journey. The best thing that can happen is you forge a bond that enriches both parties. The worst that can happen is they say no!

My stance on relationship-building is integral to my understanding of the future of accounting, which is becoming increasingly intertwined with technological developments and the future of work more broadly. COVID-19 dramatically accelerated the use of technology in business, and I imagine that the video call interface is here to stay. Although interfaces, services, and programs will likely continue to develop over time, I believe that the common denominator in business is always going to be relationships. It's up to us to build and sustain relationships to keep the engines of business moving forward, particularly alongside technology's automation.

Be the Hardest Worker in the Room

Throughout my career, I've often been the youngest or least experienced at the conference table, but I am confident in my ability to contribute. It's okay to feel uneasy about what you can contribute if everyone around you seemingly has more experience. I grew through this uneasiness through relentless preparation. Before meetings, I spend time reading up on the subject matter, familiarizing myself with the topics that will be discussed, and writing down some of my initial thoughts and ideas on my notepad. Preparation makes me a more confident and more effective contributor.

One of the best pieces of advice I offer to people at any stage of their career is to ask those around them, particularly those above them, what they read. About 2 weeks before I started my job at MorganFranklin more than 11 years ago, I reached out to my soon-to-be boss and asked what he read to stay current. I asked what his clients read. I asked what information he was taking in to inform his opinions. I started reading the same things, and on day 2 of the job, I was contributing to our work.

Immersing myself in the industry and in what those around me were consuming gave me a tremendous head start. That habit continues to help me grow. I'm always reading and learning—on planes, on trains, and every night before bed. I believe that reading and continuously learning have enabled my success. I've now been promoted several times, and with each new position I read new books to inform my approach and thought process so that I get better at the job. My creativity may be innate, but hard work always wins.

Executive Recruiting

Talent acquisition is a key strategy for growing any business. Because the market has so many competitive talents, hiring decisions can easily determine an organization's destiny, in terms of how far the business will go. Executive recruiters are professionals who bring together the hiring manager and the job seeker. Think of them as corporate matchmakers: their main goal is to find the best fit for parties with shared visions.

Executive recruiters have a stronger depth of the market than internal human resource professionals, who generally wear a lot of hats. Recruiters have specific industries and networks as their specialty—thus they recruit more effectively, saving time and money. What makes an executive recruiter successful is their ability to find the best resources to serve an organization or candidate, ensuring that they are the best fit to work together and move the organization's goals forward.

The recruiting industry is a cutthroat environment. There are no barriers to entry for a recruiter. There's no licensing; in fact, there's nothing really stopping anyone from getting into recruiting. What differentiates someone from being good or being great is their concrete knowledge, skills, and grit to work harder than others, and their ability to connect with people—there is really no shortcut to success.

Kurt Kraeger is the featured mentor in this discipline. He made it to one of the top roles in this field and continues his impact by serving on boards for companies, teaching, training, and mentoring younger recruits to continue serving clients in the financial services industry. If you are outgoing, have great communication skills, and love to connect with people, an executive recruiting career may be an exciting fit for you!

15

The Modern-Day Corporate Matchmaker

Kurt Kraeger

MANAGING DIRECTOR AT KENSINGTON
GLOBAL RECRUITMENT, FORMER PRESIDENT OF
ROBERT WALTERS, AND US NAVY VETERAN

Kurt is the Managing Director at Kensington Global Recruitment, a veteran-owned and operated recruitment firm. Prior to that, he spent a better part of his 3-decade career as the former President and Managing Director of Robert Walters Group—the global executive recruitment firm that specialized in accounting and finance recruitment.

Starting at a very young age, he took ownership of his life. Feeling stuck and insecure in his environment, he tried many part-time jobs to feel financially safe and mentally in control. Joining the military allowed him to step into a new challenge of discipline. Driving a yellow cab during college proved that he was willing to hustle even the dangerous New York City scene in the '80s rather than work a minimum wage job. He is genuine and truly cares for the people around him; I can see how being in a people-oriented business brought out the best in him. His process of trying out accounting, choosing to be an auditor, and finally stepping into a whole new arena in executive recruiting culminated in a unique journey of figuring out what it takes to become the best. Kurt has shown that he kept on evolving in different positions and roles. He made it to the top in his field and continued his impact by serving as an advisor for companies, teaching, training, and mentoring younger recruits to continue serving clients in the financial services industry. He's an example of what a real hustler looks like.

Childhood

Contrary to many assumptions that I had the upper hand growing up as a White male in New York, my childhood was spent mostly hustling to survive and help keep the family together. I grew up in a blue-collar environment; my parents divorced when I was 12 years old, so I had to grow up quickly to take care of myself and help my 3 siblings. I started delivering newspapers when I was 11 years old. After that, I was a busboy at a diner, where I washed dishes and cleaned bathrooms. Everything I made went toward helping the family. I had to work hard for everything.

The Point of No Return

I finished high school in 3 years. At 17, a couple of my friends enlisted in the military because they felt stuck in our hometown. The Navy, known as "the poor man's college" back then, turned out to be an incredible lesson on the art of discipline. I joined because I wanted to go out there and explore real life. I was determined; I knew I needed direction in life. I remember my mother telling me the day that she signed the papers for my enlistment was the saddest day of her life.

I wasn't really meant for a life in the military, but I learned a lot about myself, dealing with others, and time management. I started with boot camp, a tough, 9-week-long training program meant to teach us discipline, get us physically in top shape, and weed out those who couldn't hack it. We'd start at 5 a.m., get an hour's break, and continue until 10 p.m. It's definitely structured, but it's not as bad as it's portrayed in the movies. Out of 90 in my initial class, only 60 graduated. It was very tough being away from home during the grueling training and activities, though, and I remember calling home crying near my eighteenth birthday out of homesickness. In the South, the people were extremely different from New Yorkers. They looked at me like I was from Mars. During the Navy, I learned to deal with different and diverse groups of people. In fact, the Navy taught me the value of learning to adapt to people who speak differently, think differently, and act differently from you. You have to learn to adapt and can't take things personally.

At 21, I was a decorated war veteran. The military taught me that a 4-year enlistment, where you can't quit, is the perfect road to gaining discipline. Now, I tend to look at life's challenges in 4-year blocks. If I am to go out and do something, I go in with the mentality of trying to do the best I can for 4 years.

After the Navy, I enrolled in college and started out in the management program. Everyone, including my parents and a professor, advised me to switch to accounting. Accountants made a good living and had big houses and cars to show for it, they said. Their advice was also practical: with accounting, you would have the tools to do whatever you wanted to do.

Student by Day, Cab Driver at Night

I sat through accounting classes during the day and started a part-time job in a deli at night. The owner of the deli came in tired one morning, saying that he drove a taxi in the city once in a while and made good money. I asked how much he made and he said that it was around $200 a night—cash! I quietly made a mental note and went out to get my hack license almost right away. I put myself through school by driving that cab.

Driving the cab was a big turning point in my life because of all the different people that sat in the back of my car. This was before cell phones; I had no partitions. I talked to, or at least dealt with, everyone in some way, shape, or form. I was very disciplined and worked through the night. In the '80s, taxi driving was a somewhat dangerous job. The New York City scene was quite different than it is today. My driver's license was a wreck. I had more tickets than anybody I knew. There were often crazy and dangerous situations while driving. I even had police put a gun to my head. I learned a lot; when you're driving the yellow cab in the city, you are seen as the lowest level in the socio-economic system, and people aren't always nice to you. It was chaotic and difficult, but I relished the craziness of it all.

I would stay up late looking at maps of New York City—the city that I love. In the first year, I spoke to everyone, but the job began to wear me down and it did get tiring. By the second year, I spoke only if spoken to, and I barely spoke to anyone in my third year, but still delivered great customer service regardless. I worked for 3 years as a cab driver, and I knew all 5 boroughs like the back of my hand.

If You're Not in the Top 20 Percent of the Room, Get Out of the Room and Find a New One

My first year as an auditor went smoothly. I was happy and proud because I was in a suit and tie and traveled around with a briefcase or audit bag. I felt that I had made it to the professional rank! I spent my second year in auditing, however, doubting my abilities to succeed and questioning my desire to continue to work in audits. I struggled with technical accounting.

I had great people and communication skills, and I had a good grasp of audit concepts, but I was not detail-oriented or thorough enough to be a top-notch auditor. Since I did not see myself thriving in auditing, I started looking around, exploring other job opportunities. I live by the motto, "Always be in the top 20 percent of whatever job you are holding." Whatever you're doing in your career, I don't care what it is, put yourself in a room with everyone else who's doing it. If you're not in the top 20 percent of the room, get out of the room and find a new room. Uncertain about my future in auditing, and wanting more, I went out to find myself a new room.

While working with recruiters to find a new position, I remember thinking that I could do the recruiters' job much better than they could. I finally decided to make the transition from auditing to a boutique recruitment firm, to work as an executive recruiter.

The Art of the Hustle

Executive recruiting turned out to be the right choice. Almost immediately, I loved it. I was finally back at my best, dealing directly with people, just like in my cab. Every day was different, and it was always exciting and challenging. I'd speak to an executive-level marketer in an international company one day, then help a small startup build out their team the next.

I was very good with people and enjoyed the constant interaction. The sales part of an executive recruiter's job requires hustling, proactively looking for candidates on behalf of companies who have open positions in good jobs (the company pays a fee to find the right person for them). When you get somebody a good position, and they make more money, they're happy at work and it's extremely gratifying. The key to success is the level of proactiveness that you demonstrate: you simply have to call around to see if companies are hiring, and then try to find candidates to recruit for those jobs.

I remember one of my big breaks. It was with Lehman Brothers. I used to stay at work late into the night because I knew the secretaries left at 6, so if I did business development calls at 6 p.m., the executive I was targeting would pick the phone up.

When I called Lehman Brothers that Tuesday night, I didn't know I was talking to the controller of all Lehman Brothers. I pitched him a $60,000 job and he said, "Kurt, I make 10 times that amount. You have the wrong person." I was smart enough to say to him, "Well, do you hire people?" I'll never forget it, when he said, "There are things going on here." I quickly responded, "I'm going to be in the area tomorrow, can I come and meet with you after lunch?" The next afternoon, I met with him. He gave me 8 jobs to work on. Turns out, they were really the best jobs in New York City within the accounting space.

Being in sales is a tough business day in and day out. It is not for everyone. There were months where I would hit a lucrative commission, but the following month it could be slow or bumpy. The fluctuations in the economy and the job market really put my resilience and adaptability to the test. There were days that I would be chasing a deal that fell through at the last second. Because of this instability, one of my best attributes is that I have a very short memory—I don't tend to dwell on the low moments, and I stay focused on what's important and keep grinding. It's not just about closing deals, because a deal can still fall apart even after it's closed. People may waste your time sometimes. They may not want to look, or they're not that interested, and they can turn down the job offers you present to them. When you're a recruiter, if someone turns down a job that you get them, that may be the difference between making your rent this month and not. This aspect of executive recruiting can be very trying. You have to be aggressive and make sure you cover your entire market in order to succeed. When I started out, my company assigned me 30 companies. A big part of my job was simply getting to know these companies: finding out who was in charge, who I needed to follow up with and how often, etc. I kept doing it until they began to tell me to stop calling them and wait for them to get back to me. My level of hustle determined my paycheck, which was both inspiring and challenging. I had to keep the flow going.

The nirvana, the best part of being an executive recruiter, is when you've made the match and find that candidate that you're looking to recruit. Especially when there are only 8 people that are qualified in the position in New York and you are able to motivate one of them to take a look at the opportunity. You send their resume in and the client says, "This is perfect, let's set this meeting up." The candidate's excited about it, and the process starts. That's the part of being a recruiter where you just feel great. And of course, when they take the job. When I had my retirement party, the best thing was when people came and said, "Kurt got me the best job I ever had." And these were professionals who were earning hundreds of thousands of dollars annually. It really made me feel good.

If you're an extroverted person who can work hard and be adaptable, executive recruiting might be the right move for you. Focus your attention on people skills, communication, and building lasting relationships throughout your career. Continue to hustle along with it, and your future will be bright.

The Value of a Background in Accounting

Studying accounting not only gave me technical knowledge about how businesses are run, it also gave me options. If it wasn't for accounting, I wouldn't have been able to pivot into recruiting.

Accounting is an excellent start to any career. You can combine it with your personality and do whatever you want in life. Typically, accountants deal with historical financial information and past business issues. I personally want to work in the present with an eye to the future. Executive recruiting combined my accounting background, desire to work in sales, and vision for the future in a beautiful way.

If you want to get the biggest return for your student loans and the cost of a college education, I would suggest getting your business degree. Then, try and figure out what you want to do with your personality. It's part art, part science. The science part is your degree. The "art" is figuring out what you want to be when you grow up and what kind of work you want to do. Once you know this, your degree will set you up for success. With accounting in your back pocket, you'll always have a place to move forward. Understanding numbers and understanding business sets you up for success. Find your passion and what you are good at, combine it with a proactive approach to your professional life, and you will find that this will help you complete a big piece of what can make you feel fulfilled and content in your life. The bottom line is that if you pursue a career that you are excited about, you will never work a day in your life!

Certified
Financial
Planner™
(CFP®)

Financial literacy, although integral to personal success, unfortunately is oftentimes not part of the educational curriculum at schools. Somehow everyone still needs to learn to manage their finances. No matter how old you are, or what stage of life you are in, your financial management matters. Financial literacy can help you achieve your goals.

It is important to understand the processes involved in organizing your spending. Decisions such as how much to spend on lunch, or whether to buy or rent housing, matter. You will be more confident in attaining financial success if you understand your relationship with money and are aware of the happenings in your financial world.

Overall, this is exactly the type of financial education and planning a Certified Financial Planner™ (CFP®) professional offers: for themselves, their companies, and their clients.

Usually, when people learn that I am a CPA, they assume that I know everything about money and taxes. Many ask me questions about all things investing and financial planning, such as saving and investing for their unborn child, their kids' college funds, or even retirement. While I am flattered, I really do not have all the answers. I do financial coaching for my friends sometimes, just for fun. For the most part, bank and credit card statements are very telling. They reveal a person's lifestyle and financial discipline. Often, I am shocked to learn that, as successful and accomplished as their careers are, many are quite reckless in managing their finances. They have no savings, no investments, a lot of late fees, interest, and foreign transaction fees. Their lifestyle is also imprudent. There are so many ways around these unnecessary charges, which oftentimes accumulate without even being noticed.

The goal with financial literacy is not to find the fastest route to being a millionaire, but to become aware of where your money is going so that you can better know how to manage your finances and maximize your potential. This work will reinforce or change your habits, behavior, and choices about money. These skills are useful in life, and over time, they become intuition and common sense. If you can do it well, and teach or influence others too, you are making a difference in making this world a much better place to live in. In his story, alongside his journey, Chuck Burch is going to share with you more what he does as a CFP®, how he combined his CPA and CFP® to build his company, and the value he gains in serving his clients.

16

Guiding Toward Goal Fulfillment through Financial Literacy

Chuck Burch

PRESIDENT AND CEO AT THE
BURCH FINANCIAL GROUP

Chuck is a CPA and a CFP®; he started his own firm serving clients over 2 decades ago. As he explains, the CFP® designation is the ultimate application of an accounting and finance background. It complements a CPA designation, in which the CFP® track allows the accountant to apply his or her knowledge, skillset, and background in a tangible and practical way that could make a difference in their clients' lives. CFP®'s serve as coaches, teachers, and problem solvers, helping others achieve their financial goals.

Every day is different, which makes for an interesting and challenging career.

Chuck has meteoric energy to him, and you can tell in the way he speaks about his experiences. Like most of us, his journey was a series of ups and downs. He isn't one to dwell too much on misfortune and instead focuses on the end goals and the learning. He doesn't speak too much on how difficult it must have been to put himself through college, or how he turned getting laid off into owning his own business. Chuck merely brushes past these facts to elaborate on the doing—*what he did, how he made it work, how to turn a dollar, and the list goes on. Chuck's actions have brought about the success he has today; they have helped him navigate and explore a new path, starting his own practice and flourishing.*

The Beginning of My Love Affairs with Numbers

I grew up in Detroit, Michigan, in a single-parent home as the oldest of 3 children. Neither of my parents completed college and my father left the picture early on. My mother demanded that my siblings and I, from a very early age, be good students, encouraging us not just to excel academically, but also to engage in athletics. She kept us busy so that we would avoid getting caught up in the close by perils of Detroit. She modeled an exquisite work ethic and provided love and support every day. We didn't realize what we didn't have. We had love. We were around like-minded people who were going through the same experiences. That was enough for us to get by.

My aunt, judicious about her money and how to effectively spend it, encouraged me to start tracking my spending in high school. She pushed me to enroll in a high school bookkeeping course to study finances and learn to take control. I had a giant crush on the teacher and found a new obsession with the power of choice in finances. With little money at home, I was inspired to learn about the possibility of making a dollar grow. What would I spend $1 on if I had it? Candy? Shoes? What was I going to have to do if I needed to get some more money? Cut another lawn? Help my grandfather in his restaurant? In order to spend, I needed to save. I needed to work. I learned that I had to have more assets than liabilities, more income than expenses. In fact, my high school bookkeeping class taught me the value of a good work ethic and introduced me to a love affair with numbers.

One of the class assignments, keeping a spending journal, proved to be really enlightening for me. I was able to see exactly where my money went. To this day, I still keep track of every dollar that I spend. Of course, I do it online now. I used a book back then—a book that I actually still have—and I would record everything that I spent my money on when I received money, and from what positions or jobs. I was able to record the dollars going in and where those dollars went out.

Looking back, what drew me to that bookkeeping course, besides the young teacher, was the idea that anything and anyone can grow in whichever direction they choose, given a little will and a little time. With the right application of those budding bookkeeping skills, I could track my spending and have more power over my financial situation. As I grew through college and my career, that same principle held true for me.

Dilemma between Choosing the Best

I knew that life after high school would be completely up to me. Any future in Detroit would be spent in a processing plant or an auto plant;

I feared a future like that. I knew the value of work ethic and the power of numbers, but I had no clue what I wanted to be when I grew up. I decided to apply to college, looking first only at the big-name schools in my area. My uncle, an educator, encouraged me to apply to a wider range of schools, some small, local ones, and some HBCUs. I couldn't just apply anywhere, though, because the application fees were close to $40 apiece, a lot of money for me at the time. For any schools willing to waive the application fee, I applied.

I heard back from Howard and FAMU with acceptance and from Morehouse and North Carolina A&T with a full-ride scholarship. I remember when the dean of North Carolina A&T called and asked me about whether I'd consider attending. I felt valued, cherished, sought after—I felt like I was actually being recruited. I didn't know how to make my decision, though, so I chose to put it off. I accepted both enrollment positions. North Carolina A&T started the first week in August. Morehouse started the second week in August. I convinced my mom, "Hey, let's go to North Carolina, and if I like it, I'll stay. If I don't, we'll keep on down the road to Morehouse." I'd never been to North Carolina or Atlanta at all, so I wanted to see the colleges for myself. Off we went.

I visited Greensboro in the summer of 1978. It was the hottest, most humid day of my entire life. The freshman mixer was on the second day of school at North Carolina A&T. I was still enrolled at Morehouse while at North Carolina A&T. At the North Carolina A&T freshman mixer, I was surrounded by more people who looked like me in a single place than I'd ever seen in my life. In Detroit, it'd be unwise to stick around a group that big. Even now, I have a bit of that city edge—that wariness. But at that social, I didn't have the fear of any potential foolishness breaking out. I mingled with other students in my major, and we bonded fast over our similar passions, majors, and interests. I'm not a natural extrovert, but when you are surrounded by positivity in an environment that supports and pushes you, it's natural to eventually rise to how you are perceived. I was finally in a place where I was allowed to grow rapidly to my potential, make lasting and meaningful connections, and participate in that positive environment.

As soon as the mixer was over, I told my mother that she could drive back home. A&T was the choice. I withdrew from Morehouse. I knew I was staying in North Carolina for the next 4 years. What I didn't know was that North Carolina A&T was, and is, the largest producer of Black certified public accountants in the nation. The academic rigor of NC A&T, and the atmosphere of positivity and encouragement I received from my peers and professors, set me up to get through the challenges that would later come.

Certified Financial Planner™ (CFP®): Defined

I help individuals and businesses or business owners with the basic tenets of investment management and cash flow. I sometimes get involved with insurance and risk management, retirement planning, planning for education, making sure they are in the right financial place, wanting to leave a legacy, and any other special situations regarding people's money. We help people make money decisions better than they might be able to on their own. There are some CFP®'s, like myself, who are registered as investment advisors. Not only can I give advice on your spending, but I can also implement the plan and even help place investments if investments are part of your solution. I also do taxes for clients.

I serve both companies and individuals, which means my client base is quite diverse. I meet with a new client at least once a week and help all across the economic sector, from 18-year-olds to 80-year-olds.

They're not in any particular business or industry. I just tell people that if you want to do better, and you want to take your time, I'm willing to take the time with you. It's a misconception that you've got to have a lot of money to need a Certified Financial Planner™ and a misconception that you've got to have a lot of money to use one. Neither one of those is correct. Anyone who may be challenged with managing their day-to-day finances could perhaps use the services of a CFP®. I help people with loads of needs, not necessarily loads of money. Many times, the more money that you have, the more independent you think you are in managing your finances, and the less likely you are to be using a CFP®.

My role requires a mix of teaching, coaching, and guiding. You have to have the heart and patience of a teacher, and you have to have a love for moving people from where they are to where they want to be. It could be any of their particular needs, but sometimes it starts off with: So, what are your goals? What is it that you want to accomplish? By when? I'm blessed to be able to help them see to it over time, help them write it down, and then walk them through it. I am not beholden to any particular company's product or method of service. I work for my clients.

I enjoy interacting with people. I enjoy the reaction of people. And more importantly, I enjoy the results of the interaction that I have and what they do. I can see the results in every interaction of the benefit that my clients have in interacting with me. I'm giving them something that they didn't have when we started our conversation. I'm moving them forward from where they are. They're usually excited about scheduling the next meeting, and I'm excited about putting that on the books. When you're really able to help others, and you're able to measure how much you helped them, it feels really great. I love being able to challenge clients and help them move, consistently, to new places that they didn't realize they could reach.

I think this view is so important to me because I saw my own personal change over time. Watching my own personal growth, from the kid in Detroit to being fairly financially successful in my own life now, is a thrilling history. It's not like I had this prescribed goal of what I wanted to be and how I wanted to get there. It was a journey. Now, I use my role as a CFP® to help people on that journey, and I enjoy every second of it. I have no plans on retiring because I love what I do every day. It's really exciting to get up and do what I do. And I think my clients see my excitement when we start off doing what we do.

Not Such a Hotshot, Huh?

I joined the corporate world with an internship at Arthur Andersen and a full-time position at Peat Marwick (KPMG) in Texas after graduation. When I started, I felt like a hotshot. I was fresh out of college with options, had more money coming in than I'd ever dreamed of, and worked at a firm with a good name. Texas, in general, became a place that represented everything I did not have in Detroit. Life was easier for a while, with the security of a steady income and some prestige to go with it.

When the economy took a hit, however, I found myself, along with my entire entry class at the firm, laid off, unsure of what to do, and devastated about employment. I took day labor, working for short-term employment opportunities through agencies. I found myself in one of these roles swiping credit cards all night, testing to see if the credit card machines worked. Another time, I picked up trash on the highway. Really, I did anything that was available to me as a means to keep going.

There were no accounting jobs to be found at that time. Many of my contacts in the industry were either looking for a job, were under-employed, or didn't have anything for me. I was burning through my savings and gave myself one more month before I was going to have to fold up the tent and reluctantly go back to Detroit. I found my way out of this sticky situation with the guiding hand of the National Association of Black Accountants (NABA), but more on that later.

These things happen, and quite often. It's never a straight line anywhere, and bad things happen to good people all the time. Through no fault of your own, you might one day find yourself in a similar situation; you shouldn't worry too much about it. There are steps you can take to prepare, such as having alternative sources of income, keeping your resume up to date, and continuing to learn new skills every day. What got me through it all was the thought that if I did this now, and if I kept looking, eventually I'd get to a place where I never had to do it again. Looking for a job became a full-time job. I had to create my own disciplined practice of waking up on time and doing whatever I needed to do to get that next job. Adopt that mentality, and your successful future will simply be waiting for you to take it.

Corporate versus Entrepreneur

From Arthur Andersen to FedEx, I worked in many corporations over the course of my career, in different cities and roles. In 1985, a coworker of mine asked me to help her with her taxes. I said no twice. I did only my own and my mother's taxes and had way too much work on my plate outside of that. Then, she offered to pay me. My very first client and all I had to do was a quick fix on her income tax. I continued to work within the corporate world, but I also grew myself outside of these positions through clients that would come to me. My first tax client brought others from the company, and others from her family. From doing their income taxes, we've now grown together toward working on larger financial planning needs. And then those needs grow to their family members, their spouses, their children, their investments, and their 401(k) rollovers. I found myself getting calls about guiding my clients' decisions: "Hey, I've got this insurance need. Can you just give me your independent view on it?" We started growing together.

Over time, I developed the licenses and experience, and they developed the need. We've been able to continue to serve them. And they've been able to continue to refer my skills to other people, who referred people, who referred people. I did this work while within the corporate world. Then, I was laid off again.

Laid off from my first job and laid off from my last job. I decided to take matters into my own hands. I was the controller and director of finance for this company. I had just come off a successful tax season. I was a CFP® by that time and had some clients outside of my role as controller and director. I remember telling some of my clients that my department had been phased out of the company. One particular client said, "Well Chuck, I'm sorry to hear about that, but now you have some time for me. Let me tell you what else I have going on." Because that client (and other clients) proved to be transparent in the other needs that they had, trusted our relationship, and valued my skills, they invited and paid me to work.

I work with the people I want to work with. People I don't want to work with, who might have a need, I can refer to other practitioners. My firm gives me entry to a network of other specialists who might do things that my practice doesn't physically focus on. And then those other individuals refer back to me the type of clients that I want to work with. My company grows naturally as a result.

I love working for myself. Once you learn to love what you do and develop a love for people, that's infectious. It shines through in the work that you do.

Power of Organizational Networking and Giving Back

After my first layoff, I realized that I should tap into my organizational network of leaders and coworkers in the accounting field. During my first job, I lost touch with many of the student organizations I helped lead in college, including NABA, National Association of Black Accountants, the organization that pushed me to apply for the Houston job in the first place. They had a meeting coming up during my unemployment period, and I made the decision to go back and see how everyone was doing.

In a lot of ways, NABA was the nest. It was always a safe place to practice and fall, and that environment had a lot to do with my accounting ability and my willingness to keep going in the face of hardship. I might have been too busy to keep up with NABA with my first job, but I had a lot more time on my hands after the layoff, and it made sense then to return to the safety net NABA had been for me in the past. The pride I'd grown in working my first job had to take a backseat to my more pressing and current unemployment.

I introduced myself at the meeting as someone who hadn't been around much recently, but who had been involved in leadership in the past. I was on the market, looking for leads, and willing to talk to anyone who might have one. The ice-breaking circle came back around. Someone standing close to me introduced himself as James Darville. I nearly broke my neck turning to look at him. James was the controller of the Westin Hotel at the time and was looking for a food and beverage accountant. We got to talking, NABA being the invisible guiding hand for our connection, and he offered me the job. It wasn't near the level of prestige of my previous job, but it was a way for me to keep from moving back to Detroit, to keep myself moving, and I happily accepted the offer. Good things also happen to good people. I'm grateful for the opportunity to receive and contribute to the organizations that had my back when I was on my back.

Later down my career path, I became an officer in NABA. In fact, I was involved in many areas of the local NABA chapter and became known as someone who could help groom, make job recommendations, and help get others hired. I knew how important my role was because of its help when I didn't have a job. I would go to conventions, meetings, anything like that, and say, "Hey, look, I represent the Houston chapter of NABA. I help people find jobs. Maybe I can be a bridge to your company and the other accountants and accounting professionals that are part of the organization?" Company recruiters would call me looking for people. Even though I wasn't looking for a job, they said, "Well, do you have a resume?" I would have a resume that showed leadership in NABA, so I'd give them a resume, and from there I never had to look for a job. My role in this field helped me give back to the NABA community what they were able to give to me—a lifeline, a second chance, and an opportunity to succeed.

Just like NABA did, North Carolina A&T took a chance on me in college. I gained admittance into the world of higher education through the full scholarship that A&T offered, and I am forever grateful for that contribution. Because of the integral role that A&T played in my personal success, I find time to give back to the community in meaningful ways. What started off as a golf tournament with a few friends expanded to other interests and a nationwide scholarship fund. I realized that with just a golf tournament and a roller skating party, I could raise between $10,000 and $15,000 a year as a 501(c)(3) non-profit organization! Today, we have raised and awarded over $125,000 in scholarship awards since we started 20 years ago. It's a blessing to be a part of that. My advice is to find a way to tap into networks of support that uplifted you and give back if you can. Not only will it be personally meaningful, but it may open the door to future opportunities and increase your personal arena of success.

Academia

If there's one central theme to all of the stories in this book, it's that education is one of the most important elements of the evolution of our society. Great teachers take students through a fun and adventurous ride beyond the classroom and expose them to new ideas and knowledge. Many accomplished professionals, from philanthropist Oprah Winfrey to President Bill Clinton, have expressed extreme gratitude for the teachers who encouraged them, believed in them, and pushed them to reach beyond their limits.

Teaching is not a mere transfer of knowledge. If it were, we would all be self-taught, given all of the resources available online. An hour-long business presentation usually takes many hours of preparation and hard work; the same can be said for preparing a well-thought-out lecture.

Professor Parveen Gupta is the featured contributor in this discipline. What makes him so successful is that he doesn't just focus on teaching students the technical aspects of accounting. He understands their point of view, challenges them to think deeper, and leads them to apply their knowledge in the real-life and business world, all while teaching and passing along the practicality and the business importance of accounting to his students. Someone once told me, "If you want to master a subject, dare teach it, then you will know how much you really know and how much you have yet to learn." Accounting is just one piece of a much bigger picture. It connects to the world we live in and everything we touch. You can't truly be good at what you do unless you interact with your peers, constantly network, and stay relevant to the current business environment.

Many people assume that accounting material is dry, but Professor Gupta's students describe his accounting classes as tough and interesting. His courses pushed them to struggle a little, think a lot, and ultimately grow through a stronger grasp of the concepts. I have always had tough teachers and bosses, and I found myself thoroughly enjoying and benefitting from those challenges. His style is not for everyone, but it definitely nurtures and challenges those who are curious, inquisitive, and hard-working.

It is our responsibility to make the most out of an education—having caring professors definitely makes it a much better college experience that will serve students for life!

17

Nurturing the Next Generations of Purpose-Driven Accountants

Professor Parveen Gupta

FORMER DEPARTMENT CHAIR OF
ACCOUNTING AT LEHIGH UNIVERSITY

Dr. Parveen P. Gupta joined Lehigh University in 1987. During his more than 30 years at Lehigh, he has contributed to the university and the accounting academia through his teaching, research, and service. He served as the department chair of accounting for 9 years from 2007 to 2016. A loving professor, a passionate orator, and a kind soul, Professor Gupta has received numerous awards for excellence in teaching, advising, and research while at Lehigh. He has taught numerous courses in the areas of financial accounting, managerial accounting, corporate governance, and risk management. His research centers around understanding the impact of accounting regulation and disclosure on capital markets. In 2020, Poets & Quants, *an international publication covering business schools worldwide, recognized him as one of the Top 50 Undergraduate Business Professors in the United States. In 2019, the Federation of Schools of Accountancy recognized his contributions in teaching and service by presenting him with the Joseph A. Silvoso Faculty Merit Award. In 2009, he received the Robert and Christine Staub Excellence Award for Undergraduate Teaching, which honors a faculty member in the College of Business who is perceived to have made a positive difference in the lives of students, the college community, and fellow faculty members. He is a frequent presenter at numerous academic and professional conferences, at both the national and international levels.*

Professor Gupta shared with me his perspectives and insights, not only about accounting, but also on the state of the business in general. It is not surprising that Professor Gupta has so much to offer his students. He has overcome many monumental challenges throughout his personal and professional journey. His roles and responsibilities have been diverse: he has created a course curriculum, taught at the undergraduate and graduate level, researched and published articles, served as a board member for nonprofits, and advised corporations, government agencies, and other universities. At the time of this interview during the summer of 2019, he was traveling with his students to Prague on a 5-week international summer immersion program. He maintains alumni networks and relationships, travels, and presents at conferences. His contribution to his field, and to the education sector as a whole, is a body of work that makes the world a better place.

Professor Gupta's personal journey is remarkable. Whether it's breaking through his teaching style and cultural ideas of student-teacher relationships or dealing with the challenge of his own personal health and family matters, he continues to evolve, adapt, and push through obstacles.

What makes his teaching journey so rewarding and fulfilling is seeing the achievements of his students and the persons they grow to become. He sees his children in his students, and he continues to stay in touch with them. What an incredible sentiment! Professor Gupta is someone I'd consider an unsung hero. His impact and wisdom will continue to carry on through his students for generations to come.

A Village under One Roof

I was born into a very modest family in New Delhi, India. I was the eldest of 6 brothers and sisters. Given that my father was a civil servant, we were frugal and had a tight budget for everything. I didn't dine out until I was 16, simply because we could not afford it. I wanted to be an actor when I was growing up. I still have a tremendous passion for music and acting. The reality, though, was that my family could not possibly afford the risk of their eldest son pursuing an artistic career. What my parents could afford, and dedicated everything to, was a focus on our education. I went to public schools before making it to the top college in India.

My parents had no university-level education themselves, but every evening in our 2-bedroom apartment that the government had provided to us, all 10 of us—my parents, 6 siblings, and maternal grandparents—lived in complete silence. My father insisted on daily evening study hours. A child can't help but be motivated to do something with their time when that kind of focus and attention is carved out for them. My parents' actions and commitment to our education, along with the lack of distractions, temptations, or devices, contributed to our success.

I owe my maternal grandfather much credit for my academic success as well. I grew up with him in the house. We played chess. He got me into reading literature, first in Hindi, then in English, starting in middle school. He dropped me off and picked me up from school after my exams. On the walk back home, we'd talk through the entire exam. He was pretty good at guessing my grades from those conversations. He'd explain what I got wrong before I even got the marked exams back and would help me study to fix those mistakes. My grandfather's encouragement and support guided me along the way in my early childhood. I distinctly recall seeing the pride on his face and tears in his eyes the day I left for the United States to pursue higher education in business.

I remember as early as the fourth grade, I received a major academic award with a cash prize equal to half of my father's monthly salary. That lit a fire in me, and it continued to burn much stronger than the fire around me. I wanted more for myself. I did not want to settle for the same track that landed my father a governmental job with governmental housing. I wanted to break out of the cycle of poverty. When I finished undergrad, I started working to support my family and I continued to do so even after coming to the US.

I'm grateful that my family was able to instill the core values and work ethic in me that I could then pass on to the next generation. Those values are a currency that will never depreciate. I consider myself very fortunate that my son was able to study medicine in the United States. He now practices as a robotic urologist right here in the Lehigh Valley.

Beyond the Numbers

Imagine you're a freshman moving into the college dorm. On your way to your room, let us pretend that you run into my son. After the normal pleasantries, you ask the obvious question, "What are you going to major in?" "Pre-med," he says. You can hear the pride in his voice that he wants to go to medical school after graduating and become a physician. He wants to make a real difference in people's lives, he says. Then, he asks you about your major. As soon as he finds out you are majoring in accounting, his expression changes. He says, "I'm pursuing a major that will train me to help other people live better lives; you're pursuing something that will only provide a career for you and your family...I will have a purposeful life; what about you?" How do you return that punch?

That's the scenario I present to my students during the first class to challenge them to think about the "value-add" of accounting to society as a whole. Some of my students respond by saying, "Well, accountants do taxes and taxes are important." But if my son is elevating himself to a lifesaver, I'm not sure taxes seem as important in comparison. Other students say bookkeeping is important, but I can see the insecure, skeptical looks start to show on their faces. They're questioning themselves, and whether accounting as a business discipline really is as important to society as medicine is.

After I let them ponder these ideas for a while, I guide them to think about the ways that accounting serves a bigger purpose in society. To start, I challenge them to think about why a business would demand capital. Who possibly would supply the capital to the business and why? Since the companies that need capital and the savers who are supplying the capital do not know each other personally, lack of trust, faith, and confidence leads to no exchange occurring between these parties. What, then, are the consequences of such disinterme-diation? How does accounting information help instill much-needed trust, faith, and confidence to facilitate the flow of capital from savers to businesses? Through this Socratic method of continuous question-ing, I challenge their critical thinking skills to help them discover the answers to these questions while helping them understand the role accounting information plays in capital allocation decisions by instill-ing trust, faith, and confidence between suppliers of capital and busi-nesses that need capital.

Obviously, this is just one aspect of financial accounting. There are so many sub-disciplines within the field of accounting, all of which can be folded into this larger role that accounting plays. I come back to this conversation throughout the semester, tying my semester-long lectures to the importance of accounting. In this way, I teach accounting with a purpose-driven focus. This approach focuses my students on the "why" of accounting first and then the "how."

I thoroughly enjoy teaching my students, especially when I can deepen their interest by engaging them in debating current issues. My goal is to excite students to consider accounting as a gateway to enter the business world. Even after more than 30 years of teaching account-ing, my belief about the value of accounting to society is as steadfast today as it was when I began teaching. Even if a student isn't planning to major in accounting, understanding accounting information is so very essential to their success in their business career.

Be Flexible and Open to New Possibilities

My road to academia was not planned; it was serendipitous. In high school, I switched from pre-med track to business. I worked in the corporate world for a while before coming to the US to pursue my

MBA. One of my professors at the University of Connecticut got me excited about pursuing a Ph.D. in accounting, mentioning I had a flair for writing. I wasn't sure, but in 1983, when I graduated from UCONN with an MBA, the economy went into a recession, which steered me into academia to get my Ph.D. I completed it in a little more than 3 years, started my career as a tenure-track professor, published some research articles, and built momentum from there on. Only then did I develop a passion for working with students, helping them learn the material and the right skills for entry into the accounting profession. I had no idea I'd end up here. I thought I'd be an actor, a medical doctor, or a corporate executive, but definitely not an accounting professor.

As a professor, my responsibilities have expanded over the course of my career. I teach, research, write, and serve the accounting profession by volunteering on different committees, task forces, and boards. Aside from teaching the introductory and intermediate financial accounting courses to business majors, I also teach an international summer course and another pro bono course to 20 students on how to read *The Wall Street Journal* to help them learn how to uncover the story behind the story. Becoming a professor was a pure, wild, blessed, and lucky accident...but I don't regret it one bit. Who knows how this journey will end?

The younger generations will be living and working in a much different environment from mine. In their average 40 years of work-life, they'll change jobs an average of 4 to 6 times. Lots of young people have fixed goals, a straight line to the finish tape. It rarely works out that way. Many times, you will feel lost, wondering how you're ever going to get to where you need to go by pursuing what feels like a fruitless endeavor. You might not even know what your goals are. That's okay. Keep your mind open to change, because with change comes possibility. Have confidence in your ability to pull you through those moments of adversity and challenge. Find something to learn in everything you do. Many times, in my life, I thought it was the end. Through better and worse days, I continued to put one foot in front of the other. No matter how bad things got, I turned to family, friends, and my strong faith to keep me straight. I'm 63 now, and they have never failed me.

Growing Outward as a Professor

In India, teachers and students did not mingle. There was a line, and it was solid and bold. Therefore, I thought there needed to be a line between my students and me when I started teaching. When I started at Lehigh in 1987, the chair of the department gave me a service assignment. I'd be an advisor to Beta Alpha Psi (accounting honors society). He told me I'd be meeting with students to advise and guide them. When the student officers scheduled to meet with me, I was worried about how the meeting would go, how I would talk with them, and what I would say. In fact, I was uncomfortable interacting with them at all.

I've learned to overcome the reserved nature that I developed growing up in New Delhi. Through my experiences with the students, I realized that it actually helps my students when I socialize with them. It's okay to sit down and have a coffee with students. Interacting with students allows them to open up to me in the classroom, which in turn helps them learn and retain the material better. If you asked my students from 30 years ago and my students now what they think of me, you'd hear about 2 completely different Professor Guptas. Interacting with students is one of my core practices as a professor now. It makes such a big difference. I really enjoy their company and building lifelong relationships with my students.

Teaching is a very extroverted career, so we introverts sometimes need to find a way to recharge. Over the years, I have adapted. I may leave a gathering for up to 10 minutes just to regain my energy alone. I'm lucky to have been able to find a balance between my extroverted and introverted selves.

Drawing Strength through Physical Hardships and Difficult Experiences

In 1989, at age 32, I lost both my kidneys due to an immune disorder. At that time, it was the lowest point of my life. I really thought it was all over. My wife was pregnant, and we were about to be blessed with our second son. Then, I thought about my 2 kids and my wife, and I decided to fight it out. Giving up wasn't an option. I've fallen a lot, and had a lot of health problems in general, but I have always rebounded. I guess I haven't learned how to give up. A year later, I had my first transplant. And 7 years later, I had my second transplant because I lost the first transplanted kidney to the same immune disorder that took my native kidneys. When I look back at my health, I've had 8 or 9 major surgeries, including surviving cancer.

I had 2 sons; I lost my youngest one in 2002 when he was 13. He was a brilliant boy. That was the shock of my life from which I still haven't recovered fully. I shut down for a very long time and retreated into my work. More than 10 years after our loss, my grandson was born. A few more years and my granddaughter came into my life. The joy returned, but I'll never forget the boy I lost. That space in my heart will always be filled with his memory. My grandkids are 7 and 5 now.

I didn't know I'd lose a son, lose my native and transplanted kidney, deal with cancer, and, in between all the other surgeries, have such a successful urologic surgeon for a son, and such beautiful grandchildren.

I didn't know how exciting my students would be. I didn't know that I would find two lovely daughters in my students. Through it all, I've become a quiet, persistent fighter and hopefully a better person. I do get depressed at times and slip into negative thoughts. It happens as it does to anyone else. No one is immune to adversity in life. But through my family, friends, and students, I draw strength and am able to keep my positive thoughts and remain resilient. Every day, I see my children in my students. From that, I draw strength.

Work with passion; find value in your work—value not for yourself but for others—and draw on the power in your support systems. They will help you grow through all adversities that you may face. And reach out to your professors. We're here to help. *Seriously*.

Leaders And Executives

Leaders Inspire and Influence Others

Leadership is not one-size-fits-all. Everyone has his or her own preferences and points of reference for great leaders. For me, I remember hearing the biblical story of Moses splitting the Red Sea, leading his people into the water. I grew inspired by that process of leadership and of having others follow in your footsteps even in the midst of crisis or uncertainty. The faith that his people held in his decision-making demonstrates the importance of having others believe in your ability, vision, and leadership qualities.

Great leaders have a vision. They understand and take care of everyone under their leadership to make sure everything is "we" rather than "I." They focus on opportunities rather than obstacles, and they take responsibility, owning up to all decisions and communications.

These theories are easy to grasp but extremely hard to put into practice. It takes time.

There are many leadership examples throughout this book. You can see different leadership styles through many of the mentors, whether it is building a company, a team, or a practice, or building themselves in how they approach different problems and opportunities.

Great organizations are built with a strong vision, alongside mutual respect and trust amongst everyone, sharing and working toward the same goals together.

The World of Executives

Many people have the misconception that executives are those who dine with clients most of the time and boss people around to do their work the rest of the time. In reality, however, executives wear myriad hats, playing different roles every day based on the day and circumstances.

All employees look to the executives for decision-making of all kinds. They field questions about hiring new interns, budgets, marketing, and all other departments. As a result, these individuals set the tone of the company and the greater company culture.

The toughest thing for any executive is navigating the uncertainty surrounding the decision-making process. The information at their disposal is often limited, and their decisions have to be based on the current state of affairs, plus whatever they might anticipate happening in the near future. A combination of the information available, past experiences, industry knowledge, and a gut feeling informs the executive's decisions. This thought process cannot be quantified, but the more experienced and the more clear-minded someone is, the better they likely will be to make decisions, and, importantly, take responsibility for those decisions later on.

So, how do leaders manage to keep it together in the demanding and ever-changing world? How do successful corporate executives maintain all their energy, manage stress, and stay calm in the midst of overwhelming demand and chaos? What can we learn from leaders?

Athletic Mindset: Endurance + Daily Habits

I found that many times the most successful executives are not the ones with the most talent, sharpest skill, or largest network; rather, they are persistent and mentally tough. They are the ones who put in the extra work when no one is watching. They have the will to outlast everyone else. These unique character traits especially surface during struggles, challenges, and tough times.

Athletes are an excellent example of successful leaders. Many accomplished people adopt the athlete's mindset focusing on discipline and endurance: not only are they skilled in their job, but they are mentally tough and extremely focused. They stand out from the average professional because they look toward long-term goals and pay attention to all relevant components, intangible and tangible. These professionals emerge when the tides turn against your favor. Their ideas and toughness oftentimes position them to excel in both the world of business and sports.

Take Time to Reflect Regularly

In truth, most of us live our lives on autopilot. With increasingly busy lives, how often do we actually have the chance to slow down and think about whether our life and lifestyle is working for us? The more important question is: are we building ourselves daily to prepare for uncertainties and challenges?

We all have good and bad days. Some days we are at our best, super energetic, productive, efficient, and ready to take on the world. Other days we struggle just to get by. Oftentimes, as professionals climb the corporate ladder, they begin to create bad habits without realizing it: their actions create consequences, and these consequences accumulate over time. Staying late at the office once a week becomes 4 times a week. Sleep schedules fall to the wayside during busy work seasons. These bad habits, whatever they may be, oftentimes create unintended negative results, such as incredible stress, diseases, and intense body pain.

Many professionals, unfortunately, sacrifice the most important (but intangible) components and essential foundation of their lives—sleep, health, and relationships—for their work. I am sure we can all recall those times when we had to pull an all-nighter for a particular assignment in school or a big project at work, or a time when we may have forgotten to eat or make time for our significant other. I am certainly guilty of that myself many times. Take time to reflect in these scenarios on what you can do differently, keep track of your habits, and focus on the positive aspects of your work and life experience. Good days and bad days will come, and you will ultimately thrive by riding through these waves of experiences.

Stay Calm in the Midst of Chaos

Making decisions in business or daily life requires a clear state of mind to process and think critically. Most of the time, our thoughts are full of us fighting ourselves, struggling against our inner voice—the voice in our head that causes self-doubt. There are days I fight or negotiate with myself, especially when it comes to dealing with difficult issues or things that I tend to procrastinate. While we all have our own mountains to climb in our personal and professional life, the key is to grow a positive internal conversation with yourself, stop that negative inner voice, and keep going.

Endurance athletes, through training and preparation, develop traits and characteristics that help bring about success—perhaps without even realizing it. Besides tangible results like physical fitness, the intangible components assist with mental toughness, endurance, and discipline. And these characteristics surface especially when one is being tested during tough times. I intentionally chose Marc Hodulich and Catherine Flax as the featured mentors under leadership. They remind me of a Chinese proverb, "real gold does not fear the test of fire," as they both carry a sense of calm and optimism. They are able to think on their feet when issues arise and instill a strong sense of trust with the people under their charge. These strong characters don't happen overnight; it took years, not to mention hours of training and testing, to get them to where they are today! Their personal journeys are inspiring examples of how entrepreneurship, athletic training, and relentless aspirations can help build a career on Wall Street, and more importantly, beyond!

18

Fuel for Daily Extraordinary and Sustainable Endurance

Marc Hodulich

ENTREPRENEUR, ATHLETE, AND CEO OF 29029

Marc is an athlete, entrepreneur, and pioneer of the 29029 brand. He and his partner, Jesse Itzler, also created the brand Build Your Life Resume. Both companies promote the idea that while most successful professionals get hung up on their job resume, they neglect to improve their "life resume." Arguably, the most interesting people are those who have exciting or unique life experiences. It's much more fun to learn where a person has traveled, the interesting activities they've participated in, or the various perspectives they've gained. These conversations make our lives more meaningful and fill them with purpose. Building your life resume is one way to talk about the activities that you participate in that may not have anything to do with your job or the money you make.

Marc is incredibly well-versed in physical, mental, and emotional endurance. He explains that his job and his hobby are basically the same thing. Whether it's business or personal, Marc always emphasizes that you cannot put a price on your own reputation; he chooses to be caring and empathic toward his clients and team. Marc recognizes that his commitments to his customers are a great responsibility in order to continue working with them and for them. Often, Marc chooses not to delegate and handles tasks himself to make sure his personal and brand reputations are protected. Marc ensures his clients are always served the right way, and even knows all of his clients by name. He makes a point to learn both their profit margins and their story. Marc recognizes that ethics and empathy are important in both business and sports: people respect those who take ownership, and they appreciate being recognized and treated like a friend.

Take Action. There Is No Substitute for Actually Doing Something.

Most people assume ultra-endurance events are only for the fittest and those with substantial physical gifts. That could not be further from the truth. Sure, you have to put in the training and time to get yourself physically fit, but once an event commences it is your ability to be mentally strong that decides your overall outcome. Everyone is going to reach the point at 29029 where their body is going to want to give up. The real growth, however, happens when you hit a wall and think you want to give up, but keep going. I know and you know what the outcome is when you quit. But I always encourage people to find out what is on the other side of quitting. Lean in when it hurts. Keep climbing when you want to stop. That is where the real growth takes place. Once you commit to a goal, the exhilaration, gratitude, and belief in yourself that happens when you reach that goal is unexplainable.

In high school, I was an avid runner. I loved this identity. I felt that running competitively set me apart from others, and this uniqueness fueled me. Early on, I recognized the benefits of setting goals, committing to a process, and building my mental toughness.

I remember when, once, I quit on myself while running a race. I didn't literally quit and drop out of a race, but when it got really hard, I didn't lean in. I chose to back off and not push into the unknown. Looking back, it was a race I could have won, and I just didn't. I didn't lean in because it was hard, and I feared the unknown. No one was disappointed in me for a third-place finish, but I knew. I had damaged the reputation I had with myself, and I never wanted to feel that way ever again. Today, every time I push myself up the hill when everything in me wants to turn around, or I go running in the freezing rain, it's a little win. Doing so raises my personal grit meter and proves that I can lean in over and over again.

The reality is no one sees the 6 a.m. workouts but you. If you choose to get up and run in the rain, no one will know, and if you choose to push "snooze" and stay warm and comfortable, no one will know. But over time, those decisions are what make the difference in your life. Sure, my friends and classmates at the time didn't immediately see the results of those little wins. They didn't know how much my legs ached on the way to my early morning class because I'd already put in a huge workout. What they did see, however, were my state titles, personal records, and accolades after the track meet. They may have thought it was easy, but it was so far from it. No class or books will teach you the lessons of doing those things. Action is what separates people who are successful and those who are not. You've just got to lace your shoes up and take the first step, and that is what we encourage everyone to do at 29029.

Tough It Out in the Big City

Right after college in 2003, I moved to New York City with no job lined up. It was a difficult time in the economy, so I slept on a cousin's couch on the Jersey Shore and sold payroll door-to-door for a human resources management software and services provider, ADP. I had to move. I knew there would not be anything in my hometown, Birmingham, for a finance and accounting major. On top of that, my decision to move stemmed from the typical 20-something's desire for an adventure and a challenge. I saw every job I had, at that point, as a way to get paid until I figured out what I really wanted to do. Sales were hard. I spent my time knocking on doors, trying to get business cards, and doing things I didn't want to do. I knew the job was simply a stepping stone to where I wanted to be. In this role, though, I learned the value of the art of hustling.

After 9 months, I joined Willis Towers Watson as a consultant, where I got to create complex financial models and benchmark analyses for our clients. I worked long hours and climbed up the ladder quickly. I began to work on larger projects that demanded building out exhaustive reports detailing competitor and industry trends and started overseeing multiple management clients, consulting on both compensation and strategy.

So, moving to New York was a risky bet, but because I took action, I was able to continually take the next steps toward my goal. If I succeeded, it was because of me, and if I failed, it was because of me. I loved that pressure, and it hardened me to want to be better. In the end, credentials didn't matter as much as experience.

I think it's also important to mention that no matter what you choose to do in life, being able to understand a balance sheet, income statements, and cash flows is incredibly important—as both a professional and a business owner. Any entrepreneur needs to understand how numbers work and how their business is performing.

Choose a Job You Love and You Will Never Work a Day in Your Life

While at Willis Towers Watson, I would get together with my friends, all of whom were former athletes, on Saturdays at East River Park in New York. We would compete in 10 events, and give it a point scale, mimicking a decathlon. At the end of the day, we would crown "Wall Street's Best Athlete." Professionals in New York are mostly overachieving and competitive. Interest in our event was high. Initially, we were not trying to run a business; we were just getting together having fun.

I told a reporter at *Bloomberg* about our athletic challenge, and our entire vision shifted when we realized the philanthropic impact we could have. In our first year, we raised upwards of $100,000, and within a few years, we raised over $1.5 million. Within a short period, The Wall Street Decathlon became one of New York City's premier athletic events, where athletes competed for the title of "Wall Street's Best Athlete." Designed similar to the NFL Combine or CrossFit Games, awards were given for top fundraisers, age groups, and executive competition winners.

What started out as a challenge amongst friends quickly shaped into a full-fledged fundraiser. We went on to raise millions of dollars by creating a platform for luxury brands and luxury goods manufacturers to interact with a very niched and affluent demographic. By offering tailor-made sponsorship packages, we were able to attract a wide range of exclusive brands to our events, such as Bentley, IWC Schaffhausen, and Officine Panerai. While creating our events, we came upon the discouraging statistics surrounding funding for pediatric cancer. Quickly, we decided to focus our fundraising activities to support this precise cause. Sure, being nationally recognized on ESPN and in *Sports Illustrated*, *The Wall Street Journal*, and *The New York Times* felt great, but the most fulfilling part was contributing to an important cause that changed people's lives.

Eventually, I left my consulting position to pursue The Wall Street Decathlon full time. I loved the accountability that came with running my own company, but the expectations of constantly raising more money took some of the joy out of it and distracted me from other opportunities. I am incredibly proud of raising over $5 million for pediatric cancer research, but something about the event was missing. I wanted to not only have a positive impact but truly change people through creating community and shared life experiences. It was time to lean in and see what was next.

29029

I was coaching my son's football team when I connected with one of his friend's fathers. His name was Jesse Itzler, and we instantly clicked over our shared passion for endurance events, spending time with family, and entrepreneurship. Little did I know that we would create such a community and engage in countless life-changing endurance events together. These events were mentally and physically challenging, and also provided soul-searching opportunities for all—not just those who train year-round. When I founded the 29029 brand with Jesse, I had an unwavering commitment to create an opportunity for people to find their best selves on the mountain.

I have learned to embrace struggles in life and in my endurance pursuits. There are immeasurable lessons awaiting if you are willing to push into the unknown. I like to hike a trail in the middle of the night while everyone else is sleeping in their warm beds or run in the rain while all of my neighbors are on their couch cushions. These are the moments I have come to cherish and be grateful for. I have my health. I am strong. I can do this. Helping other people experience those same life-changing moments is now my life's work. It's about my journey, but then, it's also about the journey of all those who have supported me.

The community that we have built is supportive and amazing; it's emotional to see how everyone is really vulnerable together. Our clients come from different demographics, all with the same goal of challenging themselves. Each has their unique story, and their stories make me proud to think that we have tapped into something really special in human potential.

It is quite surreal to think about the fact that my hobby and my job are the same thing, and that I get to share this passion with many people. I am incredibly grateful for the life-changing moments and feelings I have experienced through all the events and challenges we curated.

Priorities and Non-Negotiables

Over the years, I've learned that it's important to find time for myself to improve all areas of my life so I can truly show up as the best version of myself for my family and for others. I am proud to be a father and a husband. I am clear on my non-negotiables—one is to spend time with my kids every day. I will always remember the moments when I crossed the finish line and saw my parents and my wife, each holding my boys' hands. My dad and I are super close, and he's been very supportive in my life. Now that I am a father, I love watching my boys play sports. Work certainly is taking precedence over a lot of other things, so sometimes, when late nights and travels get in the way, I make sure to make up for it when I am back with my family.

19

Balancing Acts of a Female Leader Juggling Family, Wall Street, and Fun

Catherine Flax

MANAGING DIRECTOR AND LEADERSHIP
COACH AT CRA, INC., FORMER CEO AT PEFIN,
AND FORMER SENIOR EXECUTIVE AND CHIEF
MARKETING OFFICER AT J.P. MORGAN

I have been very fortunate to be mentored by Catherine Flax for close to a decade. Catherine has a distinguished multidecade career across diverse industries and positions and has served in executive leadership roles in financial services, fintech, and commodities. Her global endeavors along-side accomplished worldwide C-suite executives are certainly impressive, but what makes her unique is her deep sense of humanity, her empathy, and her genuine interest in connecting with others.

Catherine has won numerous accolades, including Most Influential Women in European Investment Banking in 2012 and one of the 100 Most Influential Women in European Financial Markets in 2010 and 2011. A long-time champion of diversity, she has served on the J.P. Morgan Investment Banking Inclusive Leadership Council as well as on the J.P. Morgan Chase Diversity Council. Service to the community has always been a priority for Catherine; she has worked with a number of significant nonprofit organizations and is currently on the board of Cristo Rey Brooklyn, a college preparatory high school serving the population of New York City with extremely limited economic means. She is on the Wall Street Advisory Council for the Texas A&M business school. Her contributions led her to be inducted into the Academy of Women Leaders by the YWCA.

Today, she is a leadership coach, coaching the top CEOs and executives, the best and the brightest of the world, with her leadership wisdom. Her blog hosts a mix of coaching topics in business and in life and has served as a very helpful resource to me both personally and professionally. I am confident that you will get great advice from her career journey just like I did!

Youth

I grew up in a family that was far from Wall Street. My mom was a schoolteacher, and my dad ran a pizza shop. We had very little money, so I would help my dad with work whenever I could.

We'd be up at 5:30 on Saturday mornings chopping onions and working on opening up the pizza shop. Sometimes, I'd even get to help with renovating some of the real estate properties my father had acquired. These tasks were mentally and physically straining at a time when I would have rather been playing with my friends. I think a part of me, however, enjoyed the feeling of contributing something to the complex adult world. My dad would take me to real estate meetings and ask if I had any questions or thoughts before closing a deal. At 14, although I had very little to add, my dad made it clear that what I had to say was valued. I feel lucky to have had intellectually curious parents who were always learning, listening, and paying attention—who helped me foster the work ethic and confidence that brought me to where I am today.

In high school, I worked a lot as a waitress and at my dad's pizza shop. The 2 jobs, plus my school responsibilities, didn't leave a lot of free time. The free time that I did have, however, was spent mostly partying and hanging with boys.

One day, I planned to skip my waitressing job to go meet my friends at the beach. My dad, unfortunately, overheard my phone call from the other room. He listened as I lied to my boss about being sick and got quite upset—something that was rare for him. My dad explained to me that I had a commitment to be at work and that not showing up would hurt someone else, which is what made my lie so wrong. He told me, "You have just ruined someone's day." He made me call my boss back, admit that I had feigned being sick, and go into work an hour later. It was humiliating, but it taught me an important message: when you make a commitment, you live up to it. People are counting on you. It would take a while for his value of hard work to sink in, though.

Determination and Focus Is Half the Battle. The Other Half Is Maximizing Your Time.

I went to college knowing that I liked math, but unsure of what to study. I spent most of my freshman year of college as a nuclear engineering major struggling to balance between self-discipline and distraction. Enrolling in the Reserve Officer Training Corps (ROTC) meant early mornings and strict discipline, and the lure of college partying meant late nights and missed assignments. My major, and its future in a windowless room, didn't excite or motivate me to succeed. When I saw my low GPA that freshman fall, something inside of me sank.

I knew I could do better. Looking around, I envied others' successes. Their secret, which I craved so badly, turned out to be simple. They were choosing to prioritize their schoolwork. That's it. They were focused, determined, and successful. A switch inside me flipped and I decided that I would be like that too. Around that time, the chief economist from Texaco came to speak at my school; he spoke so passionately about his work that I found myself newly inspired to pursue a line of work in finance. Internal motivation spurred me to direct my energies toward my studies, take on more than a full load of classes, and continue to grow my involvement in extracurricular activities and work.

I became a huge fan of Dale Carnegie, who advocates living in "day-tight compartments," where every today is an asset that needs to be maximized. In light of this philosophy, I would schedule my day the night before, in clear terms, from 6 o'clock in the morning to 11 at night. I still do this every day. It helps make sure that I get everything done and ensures that I don't dwell too much on thinking about the past or future. My determination and hard work paid off, and after a rocky start to freshman year, I graduated college in 3 years, getting almost only As. From there, I went directly to graduate school.

Just Say "Yes" and Start Down the Path. It'll Guide You Forward.

Many young and bright professionals I speak to feel that they have to know what their entire career path is going to look like. Thankfully, though, there is no way anyone could know what their entire career path is going to look like.

I remember hosting a radio show and jumping between exciting opportunities fresh out of graduate school. I was seriously all over the place, but I was very happy with everything—rolling with all the interesting times and experiences that came upon me. I knew to say yes when I felt inspired by an opportunity. What seemed to be a random amalgamation of roles and a circuitous career path was really a reality rooted in inspiration and a desire to learn. Waking up in the morning excited to go to work that day was far more important to me than stressing over whether I was on the "right" career path. Really, there is no right or wrong path, and you can always change your path as you move along. Trust your gut, make a decision, and say yes to opportunities that inspire you. Trust me on this one.

I jumped around quite a bit after graduating. I taught at a university for a period of time. I worked in large banks, small startups, and on the trading floor. I found a 30-year home in financial services. The work, energy, and environment excited me. It felt like piecing together a giant mathematical puzzle. I started off in the commodities structuring space, moved to sales and deal-making, and eventually management. Over the course of my career, I kept saying yes to taking on larger business opportunities. After spending almost 20 years in commodities, I asked my boss for more leadership opportunities across the firm. Somehow, I ended up serving as chief marketing officer at J.P. Morgan!

That position, although certainly unexpected, expanded my horizons greatly and made me a better leader when, later in my career, I returned to run the sales and trading business. My framework of understanding for our work in sales and trading from my time in marketing led to a shift in strategy toward focusing on our reputation and clients in new and effective ways.

In the last 5 years, I have become quite technology-focused. Today, I serve on fintech boards and fill my time with various philanthropic ventures, in addition to the coaching of senior executives. Every one of these opportunities came from my inner drive to say yes to things that inspired me. So, trust me—your career will follow from your passions. Say yes to things that inspire you.

The Evolution of Women in Finance

Almost 3 decades ago, the environment on the trading floor could only be described as crude—in a fun and playful way, of course. I always enjoyed it. Nowadays, with lawsuits looming and awareness growing, the reality on the ground is quite different. It is much more buttoned-up, if not as much fun. Young female professionals often ask me about professional advancement, work-life balance, and how I managed to succeed while working in the male-dominated financial industry. Personally, I had a wonderful experience with both men and women in trading. I believe that my positive experience may tie into my ways of evaluating and responding to negative feedback, but also connects back to the days in the pizza shop as a kid.

My years working in a very bad neighborhood shaped my views of how I react to difficult people—men or women—and my ability to absorb negative feedback. I find that there's often a wide gap between the surface of someone's behavior and who they really are, and I try not to judge based on superficial things such as gender, appearance, or temporary traits like emotion (anger in particular). I often encourage people, particularly when you get negative feedback, or if something takes a wrong turn in your career (which happens to everyone), to try as hard as possible to truly listen to and hear the feedback. Focus on the content of the criticisms you receive and evaluate accordingly. My view is that on the very long list of things people may not like about me—or my ideas— being a woman is probably not even close to the top! It's proven to be quite beneficial for me to think about what I can improve on, and really try to hear the critiques leveled against me, before jumping to a conclusion that my gender was at fault for a hiccup in my career. I firmly believe that there's power in stepping away from assumptions of glass ceilings and identity politics. Don't conclude that someone doesn't like or respect you because of your identity, be it your gender, race, or anything else. Try to take their criticisms at face value, and work from there. I can honestly say that the times that things didn't work out for me in my career, it was never because I was a woman.

Single Mom Takes On the New York City Trading Floor

I moved from my home in Oklahoma to New York City in my early 30s as a single mother with 2 young children. I had no idea how life would be living in New York City, and it was very challenging, to say the least. I remember we flew down on a Friday and I had to be at work on Monday. I was the only single parent on the trading floor. My mom moved and helped with the kids for the beginning of this intense change. She was a huge help. I had a really rough time trying to find a balance between working and being a mom; my kids would sometimes sleep in the conference rooms at the office as I pulled all-nighters.

With no money, a recent divorce, and the high cost of living in New York City, my move to the city was stressful. A sense of real nervousness about my ability to afford rent, food, and sending my kids to school led me to give too much of myself to my job. I tried really hard to make sure that my family obligations and motherly duties didn't interfere with my work, perhaps too hard. I exaggerated the amount of time that I wouldn't take off to the level that it became a detriment to my kids. This may have contributed to my increasing success, but I certainly wish I had a better work-life balance when I, and my kids, were younger.

These days, I make a concerted effort to create a sense of balance between family and work life. Being interested in their daily activities, asking about their favorite thing at school that day (or work for the now-grown kids), or what they're looking forward to, for example, especially in a meaningful and intentional way, allows our family to stay close-knit. Board games help, too. The intensity of competition tends to drown out other, perhaps work-related, intensities in my life at the same time.

Leaning Toward Light

I keep myself overly busy. From serving on fintech advisory boards to engaging in a number of philanthropic ventures, I find value in investing in our society on all levels. Whether I'm meeting with a child at the school in Brooklyn for low-income students, where I sit on the board, or coaching a C-suite executive on how to get out of his fixed mindset regarding company culture, I work with a focus on instilling light and positivity.

As a sometimes overly optimistic person, I believe there are lessons to be learned from all experiences. We can always take a few extra moments to really listen to someone, smile at them, or offer encouraging words—none of that costs money or takes extra time.

In my role as the managing director and leadership coach at CRA, I get to spend my time explaining philosophies to key leaders across every industry, supplementing it with the wisdom I've gained from my decades-long career, and pairing this advice with actionable items that they can follow up on that I have gleaned through the deep research done at CRA. Through advising, I help executives see beyond their own mindsets to create environments where their team can be inspired to be innovative. Even C-suite executives sometimes struggle with fears of failure and become stressed by the prospect of taking risks. My work focuses on letting them understand and overcome their inner fears and self-doubts, pushing for effective leadership and mentorship through vulnerability and optimism. I feel honored to have the opportunity to shape the next generation of leaders, companies, and workplace culture.

Every day, we have an opportunity to change the world, through our interactions with coworkers, cashiers, kids, spouses—truly just about everybody and anybody. Adding value to the workplace and to the world can be done in many small steps. It starts with you, and your first step. Lean toward positivity, and good things will follow. Trust me on this one too!

Entrepreneurship

20

Immigrant Mindset

Building a Sweet Empire with a Dollar

Andrew Ly

FOUNDER AND CEO OF SUGAR BOWL BAKERY

Andrew is the CEO of Ly Brothers Corporation and Sugar Bowl Bakery. His story is one of the many examples of immigrants who came to the US with practically nothing and realized the American Dream. From attempting to escape 4 times after the war to getting attacked by pirates 3 times before they made it to America, Andrew's journey contains adventure after thrilling adventure.

Andrew fled his native country after the US pulled out of Vietnam in 1975. Despite several failed attempts to escape, he managed to get assistance from the United States Catholic Charity and arrived in the US in 1979. With just a dollar to his name, Andrew settled in San Francisco. He lived for years with 8 other family members in a 2-bedroom apartment, learning to speak English as he attended classes. He eventually went to college, studied accounting, and used all of the skills he developed over time to build and grow his business alongside his brothers. Their company, which initially started out as a small donut and coffee shop, has experienced phenomenal growth over the years and is now one of the largest privately and family-owned and operated bakeries in Northern California, servicing global customers with big names such as Costco, Safeway, and many other national retailers purchasing their products.

Andrew's journey of growing up during the Vietnam War, enduring and escaping, surviving as a refugee, getting an accounting degree, and building a thriving business with his family from the ground up is truly remarkable. Andrew has been recognized as the Bay Area's "Most Admired CEO" and earned the Immigrant Heritage Award. President Barack Obama praised Andrew in his 2013 immigration reform speech in San Francisco, echoing that his story, his work ethic, and everything he and his family endured is an incredible example of a successful immigration story.

The immigrant mentality demonstrated in Andrew's family represents the pride and grit within us—the feeling of seeing innumerable opportunities, the pride of knowing who we are and recognizing where we came from, acknowledging that we are tough, and we work hard. He proves that we can face any obstacle and triumph, embracing change and seizing all opportunities that come our way while making the most out of them.

Small businesses are sometimes overlooked; over the years, I have seen many successful small businesses grow in tremendous ways. Many of these small businesses generate a lot of revenue. Although the workers may be immigrants who may struggle slightly with the English language, their dedication and hard work ensure that profits are maximized and costs are minimized. It is common to see how many people who may not speak the language use common sense, work ethic, and accounting to turn their opportunities into incredible success stories. The Ly Brothers Corporation is one example of this amazing growth. Andrew spoke business in simple terms and was so detail-oriented that I could tell he approached each business opportunity through the numbers, applying the core principles of accounting, creating effective strategies, and analyzing his results throughout his career.

I was particularly impressed when Andrew shared with me the process he went through to make key decisions in his life. It reminded me of the many key concepts I learned in the Cost Accounting/Managerial Accounting course back in college, which was to understand the different types of costs one must be able to factor to manage inventories and business operations, in order to maximize profits and reduce cost. The idea of the costs (variable cost, fixed cost, direct cost, operating cost), or concepts like per-unit pricing and economics of scale, seemed overwhelming at the time, but it makes a lot of sense and it's actually quite interesting when you are able to apply them and see how they all tie into successful inventory management and running a growing business operation.

Running a business and taking care of all employees under your leadership is a lot of responsibility, and working with one's family can be even more stressful; it can also be incredibly fulfilling. Andrew explained that although it was definitely tough, their values remained the same. Mutual respect for each other is one of their most important values, in the company and in the family. It does not matter how much they disagree; they all have the company's best interest at heart, and that is all that matters. This bond, in business and in family relations, is the critical component that has contributed to the continued success of their company and that will sustain this success for generations to come.

Growing Up during the Vietnam War

My brothers and I walked to school every day barefoot. If the school was open, that is. We grew up in Vietnam during the Vietnam War. I witnessed my neighbors being shot, stabbed, and killed. My neighbor's house was bombed. My childhood experiences helped to build my mental toughness.

My father, due to his reputation and trust, kept us together and guided us well. He was from China, immigrated to Vietnam, and worked as a farmer. He will forever be a role model of integrity for me. My parents eventually saved enough from farming to start a grocery store in a second village that we moved to in order to avoid the intense fighting. I left school before I graduated from sixth grade in order to manage the store for my parents. By then, I had grown to love numbers, reading, and learning new things. I created an accounting system that helped to manage the business's finances.

Navigating the Promised Land with a Dollar

In 1979, we immigrated to the United States with no money or ability to speak English. I always loved numbers, but they became especially friendly during the time when I was learning English. Math made sense in a way that English didn't. It was hard to connect with people when I wasn't yet fluent in English, so I invested my time in accounting.

My brother and I worked odd jobs—delivering newspapers, washing dishes, doing janitorial work, and working construction. Each job required some level of English communication that helped me learn

English and save money. We saved up $40,000 and bought a small coffee shop, Sugar Bowl Bakery. The dream of transforming our small bakeshop into a thousand-person company pushed us forward. Every thousand-person company started with a single staff member, after all.

Coming to America, I did something I had never imagined possible when in Vietnam. I went to college. I began with an English as a Second Language class through the City College of San Francisco. The possibility of higher education began to seem more plausible to me. A friend talked me up to the idea of getting a 4-year degree in accounting. I decided to first obtain a 2-year vocational education and eventually graduated from San Francisco State University with an accounting degree.

One of the secrets to my college success was going to the professor's office after class hours to ask for constructive feedback on exams, assignments, and papers. Initially, talking to a professor seemed daunting. There existed such a chasm between us all, in different socioeconomic classes with differing levels of education. I pushed myself, however, to continue to reach out to them, and ended up loving to connect with them; professors (and any established professional for that matter) are people too. They love to converse, connect, network, and have constructive debates. Once you understand that, it becomes a lot easier to approach someone who might have more titles than you.

A Sweet Start

Accounting degree in hand, I decided to work for the family bakery. I took on the financial responsibilities, hoping to grow it bigger. I took routine assessments of Sugar Bowl Bakery's numbers every day, week, and month. We were a small company, and any slight changes could have made a big difference, for better or worse. It's a commonsense task for any business owner or manager, but my accounting degree gave me the skills I needed to get the most out of looking at those numbers. As I invested more time in my accounting and finance skills, I was able to apply them accordingly, watching as the business grew. At that time, we had saved some money and were debating whether we should invest in a second location a few miles away. A few of my brothers suggested that perhaps investing in a rental apartment may be better. After crunching some numbers, I was able to build my case that the second store would be a better investment.

Choosing between an apartment and a second business location is just one example of the many critical decisions that I had to work out with my brothers over the next few decades. Although it was always hard to come toward a consensus, especially considering that there are 5 of us, we all had the best interest of the business at heart. On top of that, we are family. It does not matter how much we disagree; we care and have mutual respect for one another.

In 2010, we had to make tough decisions to sell off and close all of our retail stores. We closed all smaller facilities (5 total) in San Francisco and bought 2 state-of-the-art manufacturing facilities outside of San Francisco in order to focus exclusively on manufacturing to serve more retailers. We literally cut the company in half, going from 750 different products, 4,000 SKUs, and 400 customers to only 3 products, 90 SKUs, and less than 5 customers at that time. It was a very tedious process, and mentally hard to give up many of the stores that we had built. At the end of it, though, we knew it was the right decision—the numbers said so! There is a saying: "less is more." It was all for the better, and the sales data eventually proved it too.

Accounting in Action

Everything we touch and do involves numbers—our bank accounts, financial statements, investments, everything. With my accounting degree, I am able to analyze these numbers and make wise decisions based on our company's performance. Back in Vietnam, when I was very young, I was able to keep track of the grocery store's numbers and make sure we were on an upward path. Now, in business, I use those same skills to help us sell internationally, across the US, China, Philippines, Australia, Canada, and Mexico.

My accounting degree helped us evaluate every opportunity in depth and helped to grow our business. Our company's revenue grew tremendously, and we constantly thought of new ways to serve our customers, including not only improvements that would allow our business and store operations to function more efficiently, but also ways we could price our products fairly while not forfeiting the quality.

For example, while real butter gives pastries a much better flavor at a much higher cost, many stores use alternative substitutes like margarine and shortening to lower their costs. I insisted on using real butter and needed to determine another cost I could trim to offer our customers a quality product at a fair price. As I continued to explore unique ways to approach problems, I also explored new channels and stumbled upon the opportunity to serve local hotels and the like. Most of them wanted to minimize their bakery operations and outsourced pastries buying from outside, which presented a huge opportunity for us.

Buying a manufacturing facility was never a part of our plan; we did not have enough money. I remembered learning about business planning, borrowing, and funding in some of my accounting classes, and sought help for this new project, finally securing a loan from the Small Business Administration (SBA) to expand our business operations. We started serving local cafes, convenience stores, major conferences, and convention center events.

One food broker introduced us to a buying office that would facilitate our big break to establish our business relationship with Costco.

During their tour of our factory, a team of buyers from Costco decided to try one of our products in their selected locations, paving the road for later success. Gradually, we began to serve more Costco stores and eventually became more visible. We grew over time and began attracting more big names, such as Safeway and other national retailers. Our business rapidly grew and our products could be found in many retail stores.

Entrepreneurship + Success

A lot of people love the idea of being their own boss, but being an entrepreneur is not an easy thing. What gives me hope is that through hard work and dedication, you can be successful. It takes passion and drive for the long haul, and you must know that in the short term, it will be hard to see future successes. You have to be patient and exceedingly honest with yourself as an entrepreneur, a task that is much easier said than done.

I believe deeply that financial success is not the destination. Success is making the choice to do my best every day and to invest in my family. I value hard work; more than that, I value making sure that when I go home at night, I am not just physically there, but mentally as well. It is important to spend time with my family, wife, and 2 sons, whenever I can. Staying close with my boys is not as easy as before for they have grown to be their own men; one is a doctor in a New York hospital, and another is currently in university. Ultimately, when it comes to family, I aspire toward happiness and enjoying some conversation, food, and wine...not toward being right. Whether they are my family, friends, or colleagues, ultimately, I love to bring people joy through delicious foods.

5 Ingredients of Sugar Bowl Bakery

Values are more important than a strong skillset. Whenever I hire new employees, I try to only hire people whose values and interpersonal skills align with our company's core values—family, humility, creativity, integrity, and simplicity. Human relations are like a pair of shoes and your feet. They have to fit perfectly. Otherwise, they will only hurt your feet. Hiring individuals for the company is just like buying a good pair of shoes—if they don't fit, there is constant friction, and everyone gets hurt—even if they are an excellent pair of shoes. Although technical skills matter, so do personal qualities and behavior values. It doesn't make good sense to hire the wrong person for your company; it is not different from trying to force the wrong pair of shoes onto your feet.

When I meet with an applicant, we usually start with casual conversations. In these chats, I learn about that person's character, integrity, and personality. How they act and how they talk are key components to their potential contributions. I always ask questions to get at their likelihood of success as part of the Sugar Bowl Bakery family. Usually, these questions focus on how they work as a team member, how they interact with others, how they treat people, and how they create a work-life balance.

When a potential employee comes to apply for a job, we make it known that our 5 core values are very important for all of us who work at Sugar Bowl Bakery, and we do so throughout the onboarding process. HR takes time to explain to all applicants the importance of our company's mission, values, and philosophy. At our work, we represent a family of people who share common objectives and ideas. People come to our place of work to share happiness. Our core values are so important because we are trying to help people be successful. If these people are successful, then the company is successful.

Of course, keeping up with and measuring these values can be quite complex. We encourage employees to express how they are feeling at work and have a fully open-door policy. Every year, we also send out an anonymous survey to our employees so that they can inform us about how they feel about the team, company culture, and what we should improve without the threat of retaliation. If we want to improve our future, we have to be willing to be a student of our employees. They have great ideas and advice, and can point us toward ensuring that we are upholding the values that we aspire to represent.

The Importance of Integrity

My father instilled in my family the value of integrity by living with integrity. Although he never had the means to go to school or get educated, he said what he meant, he did what he said, and he always chose to do the right thing. He provided for his family and also provided for others as he could. My dad made sure that we had food on the table and books to read. His lack of education did not matter. His integrity did.

He would bike several miles to the city just to pick up newspapers and books for me to read. He provided and cared for his family, especially me and my siblings. We were able to learn from his examples. I looked up to him and wanted to be the man that he was. His incredible integrity taught me of the importance of integrity, and more importantly, that this essential trait is a choice. Anyone can have it.

Integrity is doing the right thing even when you are alone. It's about honesty and moral character. It is essential for leaders, managers, and even team workers. Integrity is a choice. Whom you choose to hang out with is a choice. Build a network of integrity. At the end of the day, the key to having integrity is knowing right from wrong and pursuing the right decision every time. Integrity takes years to build, a second to break, and forever to repair. If you do something wrong and you don't listen when someone tries to teach you how to correct it, that is a demonstration of lacking integrity. Listen to feedback, make the right decision, and grow through the learning experience that is life. When a company loses a sale, with tenacity and creativity we can make the sale up or get it back some way, but when we allow our company to lose its integrity, *we lose the company*.

Service leadership also connects nicely to the importance of integrity, as both are demonstrations of goodwill. Service leadership is very important to my family, the business, and the people that I hire to be on top of the leadership chain here. Service leadership is not new, you just have to practice it. Read the book and practice servant leadership.

Mentorship as Integral to Success

Everyone should have a mentor. I have mentors, who are mostly good friends, and I reach out to them when I need help. Even if you know something extremely well, having someone to guide you is important. If you mentor someone, you can learn a lot from that person. The lessons of those mentees can be some of the best lessons you will learn. Learn from their mistakes and teach them from the mistakes you went through. Your friends, family, and coworkers can also serve as mentors. Peer mentorship is also a great resource. I learn from others and they can teach me new things.

Ask someone in a position you admire to grab a cup of coffee. Today. Or tomorrow. You won't regret it.

Let the Journey Begin...

Dear Accountant,

Thank you so much for joining me and the mentors on this exploratory ride into the strange and wonderful world of accounting and finance! Just as I believe in the value and wisdom of the professionals included in this book, I believe you are meant to do extraordinary things. This is just the beginning! No matter what path you are on, I want you to have the confidence and optimism to know that your dedication, work ethic, and focused, hard work will always carry you through.

As you have read in this book, many of us were pretty lost at many points in our life. For different reasons, at one point or another, each of us felt confused and distrustful of where our path would lead us. Things may seem like the end of the world at times, but in hindsight, many of the setbacks and obstacles we face turn out to be blessings in disguise that take us on unexpected routes. Somehow, things always end up okay, even if they might be very different than we expected.

There are always going to be people who will give you a hand; you just need to make sure you're ready to grab it when the time comes.

I believe we are all multidimensional. Our work in accounting extends both to business and to many other fields. Your accounting background will open up a lot of opportunities that you may not have thought about. I still recall almost 2 decades ago when I entered the workplace, I had such anxiety and insecurity not knowing what was ahead of me, but now, I am happy to say, I have had a great ride so far. It's been tough but it's always been exhilarating—and it's not even over yet! As you heard from all of the mentors, most of us took many different turns throughout our journeys, and they all led us to successful and interesting careers. Your career is what you make of it, and it may be easy to create your journey through the many career options within accounting. Humans are incredibly intelligent and creative, and we live in such extraordinary times where innovation and transformation are encouraged and celebrated. I am optimistic about the future of the accounting industry and accountants. Together, we can make a positive impact and make the world a better place for us and for our next generations of young professionals to strive!

I've always loved the quote that says, "The most powerful weapon on earth is the human soul on fire." You may not know what your passion and purpose are yet, but I am confident that you will find it if you keep an open mind and continue to try and experience different things. When you find something that you are passionate about with purpose and inspiration, you will experience a new, refreshed energy, with joy and fulfillment in everything you do, and that fire in you will carry you through challenging and tough times. So, keep that fire burning and keep helping others! Everything you do matters.

I would love to stay in touch with you and other fellow and aspiring accounting professionals in the Dear Accountant community.

Connect with me on my book website, *www.dearaccountantbook.com* and the Dear Accountant podcast. Feel free to send me a message, ask me anything. Let me know how you are doing, and if there's anything I can help with.

Life is filled with many unexpected adventures—I wish you the best in all of your future endeavors! The world is so big and full of infinite possibilities. Explore it and have fun!

Remember, the work that we do matters. *You* matter.

Let the journey begin!

Acknowledgements

I have never imagined myself as an author, sitting down and writing a book. I've had the idea for this book since I was 16, when I read *Chicken Soup for the Soul*. I wished there were stories about accountants that I could reference; I kept wishing someone would publish one for accountants. It never happened. So, I wrote it.

Thank you, Tucker Max, for believing there's something valuable in this book and for encouraging me and instilling in me the confidence I needed to take my first step in January 2019. The Scribe team with Hal Clifford, Mckenna Bailey, Emily Gindlesparger, Jericho Westendorf, Erin Sky, and Skyler White have been a great help in this grueling, yet exciting, life-changing writing journey!

To all the experts featured in this book—I have tremendous respect and admiration for the work that you do, not just in the professional field but in mentoring and lifting up the next generations of young professionals! Your contributions will change the conversation around accounting and finance materially. Thank you for the honor of allowing me to feature your story as part of this meaningful project and for the time spent sharing your journey and thoughts with me about the profession that we proudly serve.

One of the most fulfilling aspects of mentoring is being able to see young people hone their practical skills and grow their confidence while figuring out their role as contributors to society and the world. To my group of mentees, thank you for your trust and the opportunity to serve you. I am incredibly proud of you and wish that you will continue to pay it forward to serve others. Special thanks to Toby Irenshtain, who has been a trusted writing and editing partner on this writing journey, sharing your unique perspective as a college student.

To my mentors, the incredible female leaders that I respect and look up to, Catherine Flax and Tomoko Nagashima, thank you for your kindness and all of your guidance for over a decade—when I was still a very junior person, struggling to find my place and voice. Your support and belief in bringing this book to life means so much to me!

To my piano teacher, Eleanor Gummer, you recognized my talents and took me in as your student when I first moved to Canada at 16, even though you could barely understand my English. You brought out the best in me and helped me grow tremendously—musically and personally—and showed me the importance of connecting music to the heart and the world.

To my big brother, Kevin, and my good friend and coach, Israel Irenshtain: you inspire me to be the best that I can be! You are the few people who will tell me bluntly what I need to hear. Thanks for believing in me more than I believe in myself, and pushing me to write this book and start my entrepreneurial journey!

Last and the most important, to my parents and maternal grandparents, I am forever indebted and grateful for you—thank you so much for your love, and everything that you have given me to shape me into the person I am today!

With love and gratitude,

Cecilia
December 2020
New York City, New York

CPSIA information can be obtained
at www.ICGtesting.com
Printed in the USA
BVHW091621240622
640207BV00004B/13